CONTEMPORARY SOCIOLOGICAL THEORY

CONTEMPORARY SOCIOLOGICAL THEORY

SUJIT KUMAR CHOUDHARY

MANOHAR
2025

First published 2025
First eBook edition 2025

ISBN 978-93-6080-934-8 (hardbound)
ISBN 978-93-6080-999-7 (eBook)

Published by

Ajay Kumar Jain *for*
Manohar Publishers & Distributors
4753/23 Ansari Road, Daryaganj
New Delhi 110 002

Cover design by Kamal Singh Jammuwal

Typeset by Kohli Print, Delhi 110 051

Printed and bound in India

Contents

Figures and Tables

FIGURES

TABLES

Acknowledgements

It gives me immense pleasure to express my gratitude to many who have directly or indirectly raised their helping hand to complete this work. I am deeply indebted to all my teachers from the Centre for the Study of Social Systems, School of Social Sciences, Jawaharlal Nehru University (JNU), New Delhi, especially my supervisors, Prof. Nandu Ram and Prof. K.L. Sharma. I am also grateful to Late Prof. Yogendra Singh, Prof. T.K. Oommen, Prof. Dipankar Gupta, Prof. Anand Kumar, Prof. Ehsanul Haq, Prof. Avijit Pathak, Prof. Susan Viswanathan, Prof. Maitrayee Chaudhuri, Prof. Nilika Mehrotra, Prof. Surinder Singh Jodhka, Prof. Vivek Kumar, and Prof. Amit Kumar Sharma for their constant intellectual support.

I want to acknowledge the Dr. B.R. Ambedkar Central Library, Jawaharlal Nehru University, where I studied the original works on theories of sociology. My gratitude will be incomplete without remembering the Late Malik *Sahab*, whose consistent and untiring support in locating books across different libraries of JNU was invaluable.

Coming to my family, I owe my heartfelt gratitude to my parents and all family members for their unwavering support and encouragement. My mother, Namita Devi; my wife, Poly Choudhary and my son, Akshit Kumar, for their help and support at various stages.

SUJIT KUMAR CHOUDHARY

Preface

The book *Contemporary Sociological Theory* is a significant collection of modern functional theories, Phenomenology, Ethnomethodology, Neo-functionalism, Neo-Marxism, Post-Structuralism and Post-Modernism. These theories include contributions from Talcott Parsons, Robert King Merton, Edmund Husserl, Alfred Schutz, Berger and Luckmann, Harold Garfinkel, Erving Goffman, Jeffrey Alexander, Jürgen Habermas, Louis Althusser, Michel Foucault, Jacques Derrida, and Anthony Giddens.

The discipline of sociology is much older than many of its teachers and students believe. Sociology has its roots in the period following the *French Revolution* when political conflict, rapid urbanization, and social turmoil shook European societies. Auguste Comte (1798-1857) was the first to use the word 'sociology' in his six-volume work of *The Positive Philosophy* (1830-1842). Sociology here can best be understood as various perspectives and theories, all of which collectively shape our ways of understanding the social world.

My intention in writing this book, *Contemporary Sociological Theory,* is to provide a lucid, precise and accessible understanding of diverse thinkers and theories of sociology not only to the students, academicians and researchers of sociology but also to the scholars from other disciplines the social sciences. I believe this book would reach students, teachers, researchers and academicians at all levels. In this book, I have tried to maintain the original thoughts of various thinkers while presenting them in a clear language.

The book is a collection of seven chapters, featuring two major modern functionalist contributors, Chapter 1 'Talcott Parsons (1902-1979)', and Chapter 2, 'Robert King Merton (1910-2003)' both of whom belong to the American School of thought that reflects the contemporary developments in American Sociology.

These chapters highlight some of their most significant works. The chapter on Parsons deals with the action theory and the theory of social systems. In contrast, Merton's chapter covers a wide range of theoretical analyses, from behavioural sociology to the sociology of science.

Chapter 3 starts with 'Contemporary Sociological Theory' and covers the most important developments after the 1960s. The theories are either produced in the modern era/or are modern. Chapter 3 deals with 'Phenomenology' in both its philosophical and sociological forms. Edmund Husserl and Alfred Schutz are the key theorists of philosophical phenomenology (transcendental phenomenology) and sociological phenomenology, respectively. Chapter 4, 'Ethnomethodology', focuses on the contribution of Garfinkel's people method and Goffman's interactional approach. The fifth chapter, entitled 'Neo-Functionalism', tries to establish a functional approach in a new format, as proposed by Jeffrey Alexander. Chapter 6 on 'Neo-Marxism' primarily discusses Marxian order and explores how contemporary social reality can be understood. This chapter examines the contributions of Louis Althusser and Jürgen Habermas. The seventh chapter, entitled 'Post-Structuralism and Post-Modernism,' appeared to me differently from others. The *postmodern social theory* has emanated from the more recent post-modern era, is post-modern and is produced by sociologists and a wide range of social thinkers. The chapter discusses some of the significant works of Michel Foucault, Jacques Derrida and Anthony Giddens.

SUJIT KUMAR CHOUDHARY

CHAPTER 1

Talcott Parsons (1902-1979)

BIOGRAPHICAL SKETCH

Talcott Parsons is known for his innovative theoretical and methodological contribution to sociology. Parsons's analysis of the development of an analytical theory of social action and the concept of social structure was central to the structural-functional school. His functionalist thought dominated sociology during the 1940s and 1950s.

Talcott Parsons (1977: 22-76) was born in Colorado Springs, Colorado, on 13 December 1902 in a religious Protestant family. His father, Revd. Edward Parsons, was a congregational minister in Colorado (USA) and a college English teacher. Parsons completed his undergraduate course in biology and aspired to become a biologist or a doctor at Amherst College in Massachusetts in 1920. Although he later wrote much on the medical profession, Parsons was not destined to become a physician. At Amherst, he came under the beneficent influence of two of its most distinguished faculty members, Walton Hamilton and the philosopher Clarence Ayers. During his interaction with Walton Hamilton, he became interested in economics, especially political economy. Ayres offered a course on 'The Moral Order'. Parsons was thus exposed to the works of William Graham Sumner, Charles Horton Cooley and Émile Durkheim. However, the direction he took in sociology was rooted in biological studies.

Parsons completed his graduate studies at Amherst in 1924. After that, he went to the London School of Economics with financial help from an indulgent uncle. He attended the lectures of noted sociologists and anthropologists Leonard Trelawny

Hobhouse, Morris Ginsberg and Bronislaw Malinowski between 1924 and 1925. Next, Parsons went to Heidelberg on an exchange fellowship from the London School of Economics. He came across the work of Max Weber and wrote a doctoral dissertation on 'The Concept of Capitalism in Recent German Literature'. Parsons was crucial in introducing Weber to America when he translated *The Protestant Ethic and the Spirit of Capitalism* (1930). He later analysed Weber's theoretical perspective in volume II of *The Structure of Social Action* (1937). In his doctoral thesis, he explored the concept of capitalism in German social science literature with particular reference to Marx, Weber and Sombart's works. He received his D.Phil. from Heidelberg in 1927.

After his Heidelberg stay of a year, Parsons returned to take up a teaching post in the Department of Economics at Amherst. In 1927, he moved to the Department of Economics at Harvard as an instructor and taught until he retired as Emeritus Professor in 1973. At Harvard, he was influenced by Joseph Schumpeter, from whom he understood the meaning of system theory and Frank William Taussig, who emphasized the importance of Alfred Marshall, whose work marked the culmination of classical economic theory. He learned more about the nature of systems from philosopher Alfred North Whitehead. From Whitehead, he learned more about systems' character and the 'fallacy of misplaced concreteness' (Bierstedt, 1981: 390). After retiring as Emeritus professor from Harvard, he continued teaching as a visiting professor at the University of Pennsylvania, California at Berkeley, Chicago, Columbia, Cambridge and Rutgers. Undeniably, he spent his entire career at Harvard University for nine years in the rank of instructor, four in economics and five in sociology. Despite Sorokin as chairman in sociology and his unsympathetic approach toward his work, Parsons enjoyed considerable support in the university's power structure and was promoted to assistant professor in 1936, associate professor in 1939 and full professor in 1944. He served as chairman of the department from 1944 to 1946 and in later years, he became chairman of the newly-constituted Department of Social Relations. This department included sociology, cultural anthropology and social and clinical psychology. He retained the department chair until 1956. He retired in 1973, having served forty-six years on the Harvard faculty.

Parsons received several honours in the course of his long career. He served as the Eastern Sociological Society president in 1941-2 and the American Sociological Society president in 1949-50. He was a corresponding member of the British Academy, an honorary fellow of the London School of Economics and a member of the American Association for the Advancement of Science, the American Philosophical Society and the American Academy of Arts and Letters, the last of which he also served as president. In addition, he held an honorary degree from Amherst, Cologne, Chicago, Boston and the Hebrew University, Jerusalem. In 1927, he married Helen B. Walker, the daughter of an American physician whom he met at the London School of Economics and they had three children. He died on 8 May 1979 in Munich.

I. ACTION THEORY (*THE STRUCTURE OF SOCIAL ACTION*)

In *The Structure of Social Action* (1937), Parsons launched a most ambitious scheme to provide a 'general theory of action'. It is the first significant work of Parsons, published in 1937. A general theory of action would give a general framework of analysis, which includes all the leading social science disciplines, such as psychology, economics and government, with sociology. Parsons analyses action theory mainly based on the strengths and weaknesses of three intellectual traditions: *utilitarianism, positivism* and *idealism.* Parsons thought that conceptual orientations of these three traditions could be synthesized to form an adequate conceptual base for subsequent sociological theorizing. In addition, Parsons tried to make an effort to abstract from the theories of four European writers—Marshall, Pareto, Durkheim and Weber and to give a single theoretical scheme. In this work, Parsons attempted to develop a 'voluntaristic theory of social action' by synthesizing Durkheim, Weber and Pareto. The position of the British economist Marshall was also considered in detail, but the latter was largely dropped from consideration.

Parsons agreed with the utilitarian view of individuals as purposive and goal-oriented actors and rejected what he conceived to be its atomistic and overly rational orientation and its attendant incapacity to account for the emergence of a social order regulating the goal-oriented activities of individual actors (Coser, 1997: 563). Positivism was attacked for its reductionism—its propensity to explain individual behaviour in terms of physiological, psycho-physical, genetic or geographical influences and its consequent inability to account for the voluntaristic, choice-making and goal-striving tendencies of social actors (ibid.). In Parsons' view, a social theory is positivistic, which holds that human action can be adequately characterized without regard to the agent's standpoint. He considered utilitarianism as to be one of the good examples of a positivistic theory. In this context, Parsons stated:

> The utilitarian branch of positivistic thought has, by virtue of the structure of its theoretical system, been focused upon a given range of definite empirical insights and related theoretical problems. Nevertheless, the central fact beyond all questions is that human action is rational under certain conditions in certain aspects and certain degrees. Men adapt themselves to the needs in which they are placed and adapt means to their ends in such a way as to approach the most efficient manner of achieving these ends. And the relations of these means and conditions to the achievement of their ends are 'known' to be intrinsically verifiable by the methods of empirical science (Parsons, 1937: 19).

By 'rational' in this passage, he means making the right rather than the wrong choice to attain an end. In this case, the opposite of rational would be irrational (ibid.: 58). Nevertheless, rational choice is essential to the voluntaristic theory of action regarding right and wrong decisions. In this case, the opposite of rational choice is a determined choice or determinism.

Another strong tradition related to the theory of action is the German idealistic tradition. This tradition was praised for emphasizing cultural determinants such as ideas or symbolic processes. However, it was criticized for not explaining the complex interrelations between social structures and the world of ideas (Coser, 1997: 563). 'It is a fact that they manifest the subjective feelings, ideas, motives, associated with their actions employing linguistic symbols as well as in other ways' (Parsons, 1937: 26).

Thus, the utilitarian approach assumes that humans act only to fulfil a grand mental design. The idealists talk of values and miss out on empirical reality's pressures exerted on matters. Finally, the positivists emphasized complete knowledge of the situation and overtook the role of values or, errors or variations.

The concept of action is derived from the behaviour of human beings as living organisms. At this stage, Parsons was eager to differentiate action theory from behaviourism. In this sense, behaviour implied a mechanical response to stimuli, whereas action implied an active, creative 'mental' process. Thus, Parsons states, 'A theory which, like behaviourism, insists on treating human beings in terms which exclude his subjective aspect, is not a theory of action' (ibid.: 77-8).

The unit act is the most basic phenomenon in Parsons action theory. Parsons identifies four general analytic components of the unit act. First, a unit act implies (a) an agent, an 'actor'; (b) an end. Parsons defines an end as 'a future state of affairs toward which the process of action is oriented' (ibid.: 44); (c) a situation, which in turn contains two elements: means, over which the actor has control and conditions over which he does not; and (d) a normative orientation. Hence, an actor can exert voluntaristic (free will) control over events. Parsons elaborates:

> Within the area of control of the actor, the means employed cannot, in general, be conceived either as chosen at random or as dependent exclusively on the conditions of action but must, in some sense, be subject to the influence of an independent, determinate selective factor, a knowledge of which is necessary to the understanding of the concrete course of action. What is essential to the concept of action is that there should be a normative orientation, not that this should be of any particular type (ibid.: 44-5).

When all these four factors of a unit act are present, a behaviour becomes action. Therefore, action must be understood from the actor's point of view as their knowledge of both the means and the choice of ends is essential.

The action theory has implications as well as complications. The first implication is that an act is always a process in time and space. 'The category of time is fundamental; the category of space disappears. That is to say, relations in space are not as relevant to systems of action analytically considered' (Parsons, 1937: 45).

The concept of end always implies a future reference:

> . . . to a state which is either not yet in existence and which would not come into existence if something were not done about it by the actor or, if already existent, would not remain unchanged (Parsons cites in Alexander et al., 1997: 130).

Second, there is the possibility of error; the actor may choose inappropriate means for attaining his end, combined with the concept of normative action orientation. The third implication is that an act is subjective. In the words of Parsons:

> The frame of reference of the scheme is subjective in a certain sense. It deals with phenomena, things and events *as they appear from the* actor's perspective whose action is being analyzed and considered. Of course, the phenomena of the 'external world' play a significant part in influencing action. But in so far as this particular theoretical scheme can utilise them, they must be reducible to subjective terms in this specific sense. This fact is of cardinal importance in understanding some of the peculiarities of the theoretical structure under consideration here (Parsons, 1937: 46).

Again, he says: 'While the social scientist is not concerned with the studying the content of his mind, he is very much concerned with that of the minds of the persons whose action he studies' (ibid.).

But Parsons never tries to explain how a social scientist can enter the minds of another person. Here, Bierstedt comments as follows:

> The human penchant for *post-factum* rationalization of the ends and means of action should give ample warning of the practical impossibility of explaining a given unit act in terms of the means that the actor says he has employed to attain ends he says he had in his 'mind'. As a result, the actor says his action is no better and is almost always less reliable than what the observer could have learned simply by watching the action (Bierstedt, 1981: 404).

Parsons made a distinction and a relationship between objective and subjective in his analysis of the frame of reference and subjectivity. The word *objective* means 'from the point of view of the scientific observer of action' and *subjective* 'from the actor's point of view'. Parsons argues:

> A further consequence follows from the 'subjectivity' of the categories of the theory of action. When a biologist or a behavioristic psychologist studies a human being, it is an organism, a spatially distinguishable separate unit in the world. We consider the unit of reference as the actor is not this organism but an 'ego' or 'self'. The principal importance of this is that the body of the actor forms just as much part of the situation of action as the 'external environment'. Among the conditions to which his action is subject are those relating to his own body, while among the most important of the means at his disposal are the 'powers' of his own body and, of course, his 'mind'. The analytical distinction between actor and situation definitely cannot be identified with the distinction in the biological sciences between organism and environment (Parsons, 1937: 46-7).

The fourth implication of the schema of action is the *situation of action*. Under the situation of action, Parsons analyses the physical and biological sciences. Here, he discussed the units of physical and biological sciences such as atoms of iron, a small amount of carbon, etc., their constituent electrons, protons and neutrons, etc. He outlined the problems in the theory of action. As Parsons puts it,

> . . . atoms, electrons or cells are not to be regarded as units for purposes of the theory of action. Unit analysis of any phenomenon beyond the point where it constitutes an integral means or condition of action leads to another theoretical scheme. For the theory of action, the smallest conceivable concrete unit is the unit act (Parsons cites in Alexander et al., 1997: 141).

Hence the unit act and its elements—end, means, conditions and guiding norms, are relevant to the theory of action rather than the units of physical and biological sciences.

Further, according to Parsons, a general theory of action may be employed on two levels: the 'concrete' and the 'analytical'. The actual act and its 'element' means the concrete entities that make it up substantially (Parsons cites in Alexander et al., 1997: 141).

The tangible end is anticipated as the entire future state of affairs. Therefore, the function of this substance use of the action schema is primarily descriptive (ibid.: 141). A concrete actor is conceived as acting in the pursuit of concrete ends, in a given concrete situation (ibid.: 142). On the other hand, the analytical level of the action schema is related to the actor's actual capability to use and control in the pursuit of his end.

> An end, then, in the analytical sense, must be defined as the *difference* between the anticipated future state of affairs and that which it could have been predicted would ensue from the initial situation *without the agency of the actor having intervened* (ibid.).

THE UTILITARIAN SYSTEM OF ACTION THEORY

The utilitarian system of action theory is characterized by four features—atomism, rationality, empiricism and randomness of ends. The first characteristic is 'atomism'. 'It may be described as the strong tendency to consider mainly the properties of the conceptually isolated unit acts and to infer the properties of systems of action only by process of "direct" generalization from these' (ibid.: 143). These are the most straightforward and apparent modes of the relationship of unit acts and are indispensable in the systems.

The second characteristic of Parsons's utilitarian system is 'rationality'. Rationality is related to a particular type of norm for the means-ends relationship. Parsons stated:

> Action is rational so far as it pursues ends possible within the conditions of the situation and by the means which, among those available to the actor, are intrinsically best adapted to the end for reasons understandable and verifiable by positive empirical science (ibid.: 148).

The rational unit act has been described as a concrete unit of concrete systems of action. 'It is a unit which is, within the framework of the general action schema, arrived at by maximizing one crucial property of unit acts-rationality' (ibid.: 149).

The third characteristic of the utilitarian system is 'empiricism'.

> The term empiricism will be applied to a system of theory when it is claimed, explicitly or implicitly, that the categories of the given theoretical system are adequate to explain all the scientifically important facts about the body of concrete phenomena to which it is applied (Parsons cites in Alexander et al., 1997: 155).

Empiricism tries to bridge the gap between theoretical orientation and concrete reality. In this sense, empiricism transfers the logical determinism inherent in all scientific theories into empirical determinism (ibid.: 156). The fourth theoretical action system is the randomness of ends. It is considered the ultimate end of the action.

Empirical Observation: In the last, Parsons's penultimate chapter deals with empirically verified conclusions in 'empirical observation'. In any event, Parsons' described five ways to 'empirically verified conclusions'. The first of these is that in the works of the four principal writers (Durkheim, Weber, Pareto and Marshall) here, treated there has appeared the outline of what, in all essentials, is the same system of generalized social theory, the structural aspects of what has been called the voluntaristic theory of action (Parsons, 1937: 719-20). The only differences in these writers are labelled differently to the same phenomena and differences in a 'mode of a statement'.

The second 'empirically verified conclusion' is:

> That this generalized system of theoretical categories common to the writers here treated is, taken as a total system, a new development of theory and is not simply taken over from the traditions on which they built (ibid.: 720).

But at the beginning of his book, Parsons made a point that the means-ends schema is as old as the history of human thought.

The third conclusion is: 'That the development of this theoretical system has in each case stood in the closest relation to the principal empirical generalizations which the writer in question formulated' (ibid.).

In this discussion, Parsons believes that these writers can only be placed in one of the three positions, i.e., positivistic, idealistic or utilitarianist. Still, their theories become central to the voluntaristic theory of action.

The fourth conclusion is:

> that one major factor in the emergence of the voluntaristic theory of action lies in correct observation of the empirical facts of social life, especially corrections of and additions to the observations made by proponents of these theories against which these writers stood in polemical opposition (ibid.: 721).

Parsons here accepts the remarkable contribution of his four writers in developing a single theory of action. Parsons rightly points it out in the following words:

> It is, of course, conceivable that the convergence does not exist at all, but its appearance in this study is the result of an accumulation of errors of interpretation by the present author. It is also conceivable, though very improbable that it results from an accumulation of random errors by various theorists. Suppose either of these possibilities is to be considered. In that case, it might be instructive to calculate the probabilities that this might occur, considering the number of different elements and their combinations to be taken into account (ibid.: 722).

It shows that the voluntaristic theory of action concepts is, therefore, sound and that the theory can serve as the basis for future theoretical work in sociology.

The fifth conclusion is: 'that the four above conclusions, taken together, constitute the hoped for empirical verification, for this particular case, of the theory of the development of scientific theory stated in the first chapter' (ibid.: 725).

The Parsonian Strategy for Building Sociological Theory: In the final chapter of *The Structure of Social Action*, Parsons gives a broader framework of 'tentative methodological conclusions' regarding 'analytical realism'.

Parsons advocated that 'analytical realism' played a key role in building sociological theory. Theory in sociology must utilize a limited number of important concepts that 'adequately 'grasp' aspects of the objective world. . . . These concepts correspond not to concrete phenomena, but to elements that are analytically separable from other elements (ibid.: 730).

Thus, theory must, first of all, be involved in the development of concepts.

Parsons's 'analytical realism' unique feature was his insistence on how these abstract concepts are employed in sociological analysis. In this context, Parsons used to develop a 'generalized system of concepts'. 'This use of abstract concepts would involve ordering concepts into a coherent whole that would reflect the important features of the 'real world' (Turner, J., 1978: 40).

And finally, he established a definition of sociology as: 'the science which attempts to develop an analytical theory of social action systems in so far as these systems can be understood in terms of the property of common-value integrations' (Parsons, 1937: 768).

In brief, the conceptual scheme of *The Structure of Social Action* was derived from the synthesis of the Durkheimian emphasis on structural determinants and collective consciousness, the Weberian stress on the determining functioning of sets of ideas and values and the Parotian notion of moving societal equilibria resulting from the interplay of actors possessed in varying degree of a set of fundamental 'residence' or proponent-drives.

II. SOCIAL SYSTEM THEORY

Talcott Parsons is considered the most outstanding exponent of the social system theory. In *The Structure of Social Action,* Parsons focused on a unit act. In *The Social System*, the emphasis shifted from unit acts to institutional orders and the system was the primary unit of analysis. In *The Social System*, Parsons has been primarily concerned 'with categorizing the structure of social systems, the modes of structural differentiation within such systems and the ranges of variability about each structural category between systems' (Parsons, 1951: 21). In *The Social System*, Parsons mainly emphasizes institutionalized values and norms and differentiated social roles corresponding to the differentiated status position. In this sense, 'The primacy of values and norms in Parsons's system makes it appropriate to call this system 'normative functionalism' (Coser, 1997: 564).

The foundations of a social system depend on motivated actors. They play roles governed by other actors' expectations in a web of social interaction. Parsons divided this book, *The Social System* into four long chapters. The last of these chapters is entitled 'The Social System'. In the contents of the book, Parsons outlines:

> The present volume is an attempt to bring together, in systematic and generalized form, the main outlines of a conceptual scheme for analyzing the structure and processes of social systems. Like the case, within the frame of reference of action, such a conceptual scheme must focus on delineating the system of institutionalized roles and the motivational processes. . . . Because of this focus and the very elementary treatment of processes of economic exchange and the organization of political power, the book should be regarded as a statement of general sociological theory since this is here interpreted to be that part of the theory of the social system which is centred on the phenomena of the institutionalization of patterns of value orientation in roles (Parsons, 1951: vii)

Parsons's social system is built on the foundation of the voluntaristic theory of action. The social system, according to Parsons, is defined as follows:

> Reduced to the simplest possible terms, then, a social system consists of a plurality of individual actors interacting with each other in a situation that has at least a physical or environmental aspect, actors who are motivated in terms of a tendency to the 'optimization of gratification' and whose relation to their situations, including each other, is defined and mediated in terms of a system of culturally structured and shared symbols (ibid.: 5-6).

Organized patterns of social life involve the interrelation of three main dimensions: culture, personality and social system. Parsons is concerned with the integration within the social system itself and between the social system and the cultural patterns, on the one hand and between the social system and the personality system, on the other. For the integration of these systems, two essential functional requisites must be met:

1. A social system must have 'a sufficient proportion of its component actors are adequately motivated to act under the requirements of its role system' (Parsons, 1951: 27).

2. The social system must avoid 'commitment to cultural patterns which either fail to define a minimum of order or which place impossible demands on people and thereby generate deviance and conflict' (ibid.: 27-8).

The cultural system is a shared set of values and knowledge and is the basis of normative order. It includes the norms and roles of the societal action system. The personality system integrates the individual's various roles and biological needs. This personality element motivates the actions of individuals. The social system is the system of actual interactions among the plurality of actors. Social life involves the relationships between individuals. These social relationships contribute to the elements of the 'social system'. Hence, roles coordinate actions and choices by linking these three systems. For instance, social systems and personalities are shaped by culture, while culture (shared ideas) has to be rooted in individuals (characters) and social relationships (social systems). Therefore, Parsonian analysis concerns how these three elements interrelate and how they 'integrate' into the working pattern in any social setting.

There are various integrating forces and mechanisms, but in Parsons's view, the primary and necessary tool is internalizing cultural standards and values in individual personalities. However, Parsons recognizes that cultural values are never perfectly internalized and shared and are only partially consistent and integrated as a system. In this sense, Parsons pointed out the integrative problems of articulating culture and the personality system with the social system. At this juncture, the concept of institutionalization is essential to the conceptualization of the social system. Institutionalization is the expression of cultural values in interaction.

Parsons views institutionalization as both a process and a structure. As a process, institutionalization can be discussed in the following way:

(1) Actors who are variously oriented enter into situations where they must interact. (2) The way actors are oriented is a reflection of their need structure and how the internalization of cultural patterns has altered this need structure.

(3) Through specific interaction processes not indicated by implication, including role-taking, role bargaining and exchange, norms emerge as actors adjust their orientations to each other. (4) Such norms emerge as a way of adjusting actors' orientations to each other, but, at the same time, they are circumscribed by general cultural patterns. (5) These norms regulate subsequent interaction, giving it stability. Institutionalized patterns are created, maintained and altered (Turner, J, 1978: 47).

The 'structure of social systems consists of institutionalized normative culture in the action frame of reference' (Parsons, 1961: 37). Therefore, only the institutionalized normative expectations make up the structure of social systems. In brief, institutionalization is the process through which social structure is built and maintained.

BASIC UNIT OF ORGANIZATION OF A SOCIAL SYSTEM

The process involves a mode of organization of action in the social system called *role.* The role is the basic conceptual unit of the social system that coordinates actions and choices by linking three social, cultural and personality systems. According to Parsons, the role's primary element is *role expectation.* It implies reciprocity between the individual actor and the other persons. A range of motivational and value orientations governs it.

Motivational orientation refers to a situation in which action takes place considering the individual actors' needs or motives, external appearances and plans. In other words, it supplies the energy, i.e., 'an urge to get something' (Abraham and Francis, 2000: 53-4).

There are three motivational orientations—cognitive, cathectic, and evaluative.

(i) *Cognitive orientation* refers to the belief that cognitive meanings imply what is or what the actors perceive (ibid.: 54). In this sense, actors try to see their environ-ment or object concerning their needs.
(ii) The *cathectic orientation* involves actors' sentimental and emotional attitudes towards their object. In this sense, the actor perceives what is pleasurable or painful (ibid.).

(iii) The *evaluative orientation* involves the judgement and interpretation of alternatives and the selection of appropriate means (ibid.).

On the other hand, value orientation refers to observing social norms or standards (ibid.). It involves the organization of the unit acts into social systems.

> The value orientation supplies norms or standards of action. Internalized, they are need-disposition within actors, institutionalized in the social system and contribute to integration, abstracted from the concrete situation and cultural value standards (Loomis and Loomis, 1965: 331).

The range of value orientation also comprises three parts, i.e., the cognitive, the appreciative and the moral.

(i) The *cognitive orientation* relates to the issue of the validity of the judgement.
(ii) The *appreciative orientation* allows actors to judge their emotional response to an object.
(iii) *Moral orientation* is that which is neither cognitive nor appreciative. Still, it involves synthesizing both aspects and 'constitutes the standards in which more particular evaluations are themselves evaluated' (Parsons, 1951: 13-14). In this way, moral orientation is related to the value commitment of an actor towards their objects.

Motivational orientation and value orientation are two orientations that define role and role expectations' behavioural and cultural aspects. In addition, Parsons identifies three types of action in connection with the basic unit of organization of a social system:

1. *Instrumental action:* 'This is oriented to achieving a goal which is an anticipated future state of affairs and gives primacy to the cognitive model of orientation' (Abraham and Francis, 2000: 54).
2. *Expressive action:* Here, 'the primary orientation is not to attain a goal anticipated for the future, but the organization of the "flow" of gratification' (Parsons, 1951: 49).

This type of action is a goal and prioritizes the cathectic mode of orientation.

3. *Moral action:* Here 'the focus is on the system of the order itself, not on the goals transcendent to it nor the gratification interests of the actor. This may be called the "moral" aspect of the ordering of action and the cultural values that have priority with it; moral values . . . the social system focus . . . may be called the "relational" orientation of action while that to the integration of personality may be called the "ego-integrative"' (Parsons, 1951: 50).

III. FUNCTIONAL PREREQUISITES OR REQUIREMENTS

To understand Parsons's analysis of the integration of systems and his approach to functional requirements, we must discuss his approach to the notion of survival. In this context, two conditions in any system must be met to survive. First, it must relate effectively to its environment and maintain its internal integrity. Parsons further breaks down these two vital conditions into 'four imperatives or prerequisites or requirements', which any system must satisfy. These four prerequisites appear in Edward A. Shils, Robert Freed Bales and Talcott Parsons's major work, *Working Papers in the Theory of Action* (1953). Parsons outlines the basic theme of functional requirements in his own words:

> In light of subsequent development, the crucial outcome was the emergence of what we now call the 'four-function paradigm'. In his Interaction Process Analysis, its genesis converges between the four elementary pattern variables and Bales' classification (Bales, 1950). As a result, we concluded that systems of action generally could be exhaustively analyzed in terms of processes and structures referable to the solution—simultaneously or in sequence—of the four functional problems that we called 'adaptation,' 'system (not unit) goal attainment', 'integration' and 'pattern-maintenance and latent tension-management'. Though there were many defects in our formulations at that time, this primary classification has remained with me for more than fifteen years since it first emerged and has constituted a primary reference point of all my theoretical work (Parsons, 1977: 43).

The four functional requisites are developed, called the 'A, G, I, L or AGIL' scheme. With the introduction of the AGIL scheme, there is a shift away from analysing structures to analysing functions. Parsons believes that four fundamental functions must be performed in every social system. Parsons outlines it in the following words:

> The basic functional problems of systems of action we have formulated are (1) 'adaptation', i.e., to objects in the situation outside the system, (2) 'goal-attainment', i.e., the establishment of 'consummatory' relations to situational objects by 'instrumental' processes, (3) 'integrative', the maintenance of a state of internal 'harmony' or absence of 'conflict' among the units of the system, and (4) 'Latent pattern-maintenance and tension-management', the maintenance both of the structure of the internalized-institutionalized normative or cultural patterns and motivation to conformity with their requirements (Parsons, 1953: 624-5).

In addition to four functional requirements, based on the above statement, we find two more dichotomies: external-internal and instrumental-consummatory contradiction. The instrumental refers to activity representing the means to a goal, while consummatory involves achieving some desired and, i.e., end. Conversely, the external-internal dichotomy depends on whether the action is oriented toward a social system's external or internal situation. Thus, we begin with four functional requirements for detailed analysis and its relation to various social institutions.

1. *Adaptation:* It involves securing the environment with sufficient facilities and then distributing these facilities throughout the system (Turner, J., 1978: 51). Any society, therefore, must be able to mobilize resources to get things done. It must extract the necessary facilities for collective action from its environment. For instance, there is the need to extract resources from the physical environment, such as food, shelter, etc. In the economic system, the primary functions are resource utilization, production and distribution in the society that people need to live and carry out their social responsibilities. Therefore, adaptation is an external factor to the system and has an instrumental character.

2. *Goal-attainment:* It refers to the problem of establishing priorities among system goals and mobilizing system resources for their attainment (ibid.). The function of goal attainment is to maximize the society's capacity to attain collective goals. The

organization of the power and authority, i.e., institutions of government (Polity), has a primary role in achieving collective goals. Thus, goal attainment has a consummatory character and involves external interaction.

Therefore, adaptation and goal attainment refers to the first condition of survival, the need for social units to relate to the environment from which they draw facilities and inject 'outputs' of those achievements.

3. *Integration:* It denotes the problem of coordinating and maintaining possible interrelationships among system units (ibid.). There are possibilities of strain and conflict, so there must be ways to regulate relations amongst parts and prevent difficulties from getting out of hand. In the social system, the function of integration is mainly performed by culture and values. Therefore, community and cultural institutions, such as organized religion, education and mass communication, serve the function of integration. In this process, the 'social control' mechanism is also used. The police and courts play prominent roles here. This functional prerequisite is internal to the system and has a consummatory character.

4. *Pattern maintenance and tension management (Latency):* Latency involves two problems—pattern maintenance and tension management.

> Pattern maintenance pertains to the problem of how to ensure that actors in the social system display the 'appropriate' characteristics (motives, needs, role-playing skills and so forth). Tension management concerns the problem of dealing with the internal tensions and strains of actors in the social system (ibid.).

Latency tries to maintain the structural patterns of the institutionalized culture of the system, especially its fundamental values. For example, the family mainly handles the latency problems through the members' socialization process. Within a family, children are brought up in the culture and ways of the society (thereby providing pattern maintenance); the relations of affection, companionship, joint participation in leisure, etc., amongst the members offer comfort, consolation and relief (thereby dealing with tension management). Thus, the functional prerequisite of latency bears an instrumental character within the system. Parsons's analysis of 'Functional Prerequisites' can be presented in Table 1.1.

TABLE 1.1: FUNCTIONAL PREREQUISITES OF A SOCIAL SYSTEM

	Instrumental	*Consummatory*
External	Adaptation Economic system—resource utilization, production, distribution, etc. The primary subsystems—factory system, the banking system	Goal Attainment Political system—State Major subsystems—Political Parties, bureaucracies
Internal	Latency Family, Socialization Prominent subsystem—nuclear family, marriage	Integration Cultural and Community System—Religion, Media Primary subsystem—schools, churches, ideology.

However, in many societies, we do not find specialized social agencies such as courts, businesses, parliaments, etc. Instead, these types of society are mainly characterized by a kinship system and regulated by economic activity, political interaction, the socialization and education of the young, religious rituals and control and punishment of the offender. In this sense, the four functional requirements must be satisfied in such a society, but they must still be met by specialized means.

IV. PATTERN VARIABLES OR VALUE DILEMMAS

The different specific functions, i.e., adaptation, goal-attainment, integration and latency, can be met by many other specific institutionalized patterns in the various types of human society. For example, obtaining food, an instance of adaptation, can be done by hunting and gathering. The term *pattern variables* is used to categorize the modes of orientation in personality systems., the value patterns of culture and the normative requirements in social systems. These pattern variables are polar dichotomies.

Parsons's pattern variables are based on Ferdinand Toennies' *gemeinschaft-gesellschaft*. Toennies was interested in constrasting primitive communities (*gemeinschaft*) with industrial (*gesellschaft*) societies. Parsons, like Toennies, considers the difference between the two fundamental. He labels relationships in traditional societies as 'expressive' and relationships in modern societies as 'instrumental'. Parsons's pattern variables, however, are a fivefold elaboration of the traditional-modern typology in place of a simple twofold typology. Parsons defines pattern variables as 'a dichotomy, one side of which must be chosen by an actor before the meaning of a situation is determinate for him and thus before he can act concerning that situation' (Parsons, 1951: 77).

In other words, each pattern variable represents a problem or dilemma the actor must solve before taking action.

Table 1.2 represents the pattern variable scheme. In each case, the choices actors appropriately make a difference according to the type of society. The appropriate choices for traditional societies are on the left-hand side (expressive) and the appropriate choices for modern societies are on the right-hand side (instrumental).

The first choice actors make between ascription and achievement is also labelled as 'quality' and 'performance'. This dilemma deals with the issue of whether an actor is oriented toward others based on inborn qualities, such as sex, age, race and family status or based on performance. For example, in traditional society, racial discrimination and caste superiority are based on quality or ascription rather than achievement or performance. Therefore, ascriptions are based on assigning particular attributes to a person by birth, age, sex, kinship or race. Another example 'in modern societies, employers are expected to orient themselves toward potential employees based on the work they have done in the past and that they could be expected to do in the future, not according to their colour, age, sex or family connections. Thus, employers should choose the performance or achievement side of the pattern variable dichotomy rather than the ascriptive or quality side' (Wallace and Wolf, 1980: 24). Achievement is, therefore, based

TABLE 1.2: PARSONS' PATTERN VARIABLES (CUFF, SHARROCK AND FRANCIS, 1990: 50)

Pattern Variable A	*Pattern Variable B*
Expressive (gemeinschaft) An emphasis on emotional satisfaction	*Instrumental (gesellschaft)* A focus on achieving goals and accomplishing tasks.
Ascription Emphasizing the qualities or attributes of actors, i.e., who they are.	*Achievement* Emphasis on the performance of actors, i.e., what they do.
Diffuseness Emphasis on broad relationships deals with various purposes and interests, e.g., the relationship between a mother and a child.	*Specificity* Emphasizing limited relationships for specific purposes, e.g., the relationship between a doctor and a patient.
Particularism Emphasizing the organization of particular relationships with particular actors, e.g., 'being loyal to one's mother'.	*Universalism* Emphasize the organization of interaction according to general principles, e.g., treating everyone equally before the law.
Affectivity Emphasizing the gratification of emotions.	*Affective Neutrality* Emphasizing the postponement of gratification, i.e., disciplining oneself.
Collective Orientation Emphasizing collectivism, i.e., pursuing shared interests.	*Self-Orientation* Emphasizing individualism, i.e., pursuing private interests.

on the personal acquisition of skills and the levels of performance in society.

The second pattern variable is *diffuseness* and *specificity*. This 'is the dilemma of defining the relation borne by an object to the actor as indefinitely wide in scope, infinitely broad in involvement, morally obligating and significant in pluralistic situations (diffuseness); or specifically limited in scope and involvement (specificity)' (Loomis and Loomis, 1965: 342).

In other words, if the number and types of demands or responsibilities are wide-ranging, it is a diffuse relationship; if the scope is narrow or very limited, the relationship is functionally specific (Wallace and Wolf, 1980: 24). For instance, the relationship between doctors and patients, buyers and sellers of goods in the market or between the employer and employees in a modern factory system has a particular scope. On the contrary, they are very general and encompassing in nature. Such relations are friendships, the conjugal relationship between husband and wife and relationships between kin of various degrees. These relationships are diffuse. In specificity, the relationship has no obligation, while it involves a 'limitless' number of commitments in diffuseness.

The third pattern variable is *particularism* and *universalism.* In this dilemma, 'normative expectations must reflect a proper balance between specific applicability to certain types of actors and specific situations and universally applicable principles' (Handel, 1993: 25).

In other words, in particularism, an actor chooses a particular object based on specific relations, while in universalism, the choice is made based on the general norm. Thus, teachers' attitudes toward all students are considered 'impartial and equal' based on universalistic criteria. But if the same teacher favours his son, who happens to be in the same class, he behaves particularistically. 'In general, questions of "discrimination" involve choices based on particularistic criteria rather than the universalistic criteria that modern societies believe in and prescribe' (Wallace and Wolf, 1980: 25).

In short, universalism or particularism is a pattern variable that defines the role of the actor's dilemma between the cognitive versus the cathectic (or emotional standard) evaluation.

The fourth pattern variable is *affective* and *affective neutrality.* This dilemma concerns the appropriate emotion or effects in a given interaction situation. For example,

> The pattern is effective when an organized action system emphasizes gratification, that is, when an actor tries to avoid pain and to maximize pleasure, the pattern is effectively neutral when it imposes discipline and renouncement of deferment of some gratifications in favour of other interests (Abraham and Francis, 2000: 58).

For example, an engaged couple can undoubtedly expect to relate to each other with affectivity. On the other hand, a high school teacher and student are related to affective neutrality.

The fifth pattern variables are *collective orientation* and *self-orientation.* This dilemma 'denotes the extent to which action is to be oriented to self-interest and individual goals or group interests and goals' (Turner, J., 1978: 48).

The dilemma of this pattern variable is present in human life from the primitive mode of economy and society to modern civilization. A socialist society is an excellent example of collective orientation. The work of shopkeepers and salespeople is considered self-oriented.

According to Parsons, the pattern variables provide an overview of the nature of role interaction and role expectations in a social system and give us a direction in which most social system members choose their roles. For instance, the role expectation within the family, as a social system, amongst its members can be said to be affective, collectively-oriented, particularistic, ascriptive and diffuse. On the other hand, a student's role expectation and role performance in a student association would be oriented towards affective neutrality, self-orientation, universalism, achievement and specificity pattern variables. The pattern variables falling in the 'expressive' category are likely to occur together, as are those falling in the 'instrumental' category. For example, universalism is very similar to achievement or performance; particularism is similar to ascription or quality.

V. FUNCTIONALISM

Parsons, a leading proponent of functionalist theory, viewed society as naturally being in a state of equilibrium. By 'equilibrium', he meant that society tends toward a state of stability and balance. Therefore, Parsons tried constructing a simple equilibrium model that develops in social relations through the idea of 'shared expectations'. According to his equilibrium model, as changes occur in one part of society, there must be adjustments in other parts. If this does not happen, society's equilibrium will be threatened and strains will occur.

The central point of his functionalism is the question of how social order is possible. He observes that social life is characterized by 'mutual advantage and peaceful cooperation rather than mutual hostility and destruction' (Haralambos, 1999: 526).

His functional approach focuses on the importance of values and norms to social organization. Value consensus plays a crucial role in the integration of society. In this context, shared values are essential. Norms are specific expressions of values. Parsons argues that 'the rules of the society, its norms of proper conduct, become the expectations of its members' (Cuff, Sharrock and Francis, 1990: 46). Therefore, Parsons is interested in how the norms and values are transferred to the actors within the system. At this point, the concept of role and socialization got the position in his functionalist approach. As Parsons puts it, 'The combination of value orientation patterns which is acquired (by the actor in socialization) *must in a significant degree be a function of the fundamental role structure and dominant values of the social system*' (Parsons, 1951: 227).

Parsons's notion of 'value consensus' led him to state that the main task of sociology is to analyse the 'institutionalization of patterns of value orientation in the social system'. He emphasized that institutionalization is necessary for integration and is an essential means of achieving it. Hence, a state of 'social equilibrium' is attained and the various parts of the system are balanced—two main ways to maintain social equilibrium: socialization and social control. As Haralombus puts it,

> The first involves socialization by means of which society's values are transmitted from one generation to the next and internalized to form an integral part of individual personalities . . . social equilibrium is also maintained by the various mechanisms of social control which discourage deviance and so maintain order in the system. Thus, the process of socialization and social control are fundamental to the equilibrium of the social system and therefore to order in society (Haralambos, 1999: 528).

Parsons sees socialization as a lifelong process. People learn expectations from one another in socialization. In this way, people become attached to social rules and feel that they and others ought to behave in the way they are expected to behave. In abstract terms, mechanisms of socialization are seen by Parsons as the means through which cultural patterns are internalized into the personality system (Turner, J., 1978: 49). Conversely, social control mechanisms involve organizing status roles in social systems to reduce strain and deviance (ibid.: 50).

In the functional approach, Parsons argues that any social system has four essential functional prerequisites—adaptation, goal-attainment, integration, and latency (for details, see under the heading of functional requirements or prerequisites). In addition, Parsons identifies four mechanisms through which integration is enhanced and social order is maintained.

> First is *integrative communication*—the sharing of information. The second is ritual, which expresses commitment or loyalty to the group and its values. The third is *permissiveness*—allowing limited amounts of diversity enhances integration. . . . Fourth, there is mutual support (Handel, 1993: 27).

Functionalism has often been criticized for not providing an adequate explanation for social change. In equilibrium, the various parts of the system are in order and stable; hence, it is difficult to see how it changes at this juncture. However, Parsons tries to solve this problem with the help of the concept of *moving equilibrium.* Parsons believes that moving equilibrium is a more appropriate concept to understand societal changes rather than stable equilibrium. This is because the human organism constantly changes in developing from the body into an adult. Still, throughout the changes, it retains its unity and identity and it is the same with societies too (Cuff, Sharrock and Francis, 1990: 47). Societies change by altering functional requirements—such as adaptation, goal-attainment, integration and latency—yet they develop without disintegrating. Thus, the equilibrium of a social system is 'moving' rather than 'stable'. In this way, social systems never attain stable or complete equilibrium; hence, social change can be seen in terms of 'moving equilibrium'.

VI. CYBERNETIC HIERARCHY OF CONTROL

The cybernetic hierarchy of control is a conceptual scheme of Parsons for classifying the locus of social change. According to him, the information energic interchanges among action systems provide the potential for the difference within or between the action systems. 'One source of change may be excesses in either information or energy in the exchange among action systems, which, in turn, alter the informational or energic outputs across systems and within any system' (Turner, J., 1978: 56).

At the end of the 1950s, Parsons tried to make interrelationships among four distinct action systems: culture, society, personality and organism. The social system is the integrative subsystem of action in general. The other three systems, i.e., culture, personality and organism constitute the social system. Parsons believes all action systems have constituent subsystems (Parsons, 1961: 30-8). In this context, Loomis has effectively summarized the relationship between the systems and subsystems as follows:

> Organization and control are exhibited by one ordering of levels of the four systems. The psychological system organizes and controls the organism (in its behavioural aspects); the social system organizes and controls the psychological system. The cultural system performs similarly with respect to the social system. By an opposite ordering of the levels, sets of conditions basic to the cultural system, psychological systems are a set of conditions on which the social systems depend and the organism provides the psychological system's conditions. There are characteristic interchanges among the four systems. The organism, for example, provides the personality system with inputs of motivational energy, part of which is fed back to the organism in the form of control that increases the performance potential of the organism. Between the psychological and cultural systems, a mutually integrative interchange occurs in which the psychological system is provided with legitimation by cultural components. Its functioning is subject to normative patterns. Culture is provided with a 'motivational commitment' by the psychological system, which transcends an understanding of the norm to become a total internalization of it. The norm becomes part of an integral regulatory mechanism that is part of the personality system itself (Loomis and Loomis, 1968: 332-3).

The overall action system and each of the subsystems fulfilling one of the four system functional requirements—adaptation, goal-attainment, integration and latency—are described by Turner as follows:

> The organism is considered the subsystem is having the most consequences for resolving adaptive problems. It is ultimately through this system that environmental resources are made available to the other action subsystems. As the goal-seeking and decision-making system, personality is considered

to have primary consequences for resolving goal-attainment problems. As an organized network of status-norms integrating the patterns of the cultural system and the needs of personality systems, the social system is viewed as the major integrative subsystem of the general action system. As the repository of the symbolic content of the interaction, the cultural system is considered to have primary consequences for managing tensions of actors and assuring that the proper symbolic resources are available to ensure institutional patterns' maintenance (Latency) (Turner, J., 1978: 53-4).

Each action system (i.e., organism, personality or culture) devotes itself to a social subsystem in the overall action system. According to Parsons, one subsystem affects the other in the hierarchy of informational control.

> What emerges in a hierarchy of informational controls, with culture informationally circumscribing the social system, social structure informationally regulating the personality system and personality informationally regulating the organic system. (ibid.: 54).

For instance, culture-based value orientations control the norms of the social system. In turn, these norms would control the motives and decision-making processes in the personality system. Finally, these feature personality system features would affect the organism's biochemical process and entire scheme of 'cybernetic hierarchy' is explained by Turner in the following words:

> . . . each system in the hierarchy is also viewed as providing the 'energic conditions' necessary for action at the next higher system. Thus, the organism provides the energy necessary for the personality system. The personality system provides the energic conditions for the social system and the organization of personality systems into a social system offers the conditions necessary for a cultural system. Thus, the input-output relations among action systems are reciprocal, with systems exchanging information and energy. Systems high in information circumscribe the utilization of energy at the next lower system level. In contrast, each lower system provides the conditions and facilities necessary for action in the next higher system. This scheme has been termed a 'cybernetic hierarchy' (ibid.: 54-5).

The entire scheme of the cybernetic hierarchy of control can be represented diagrammatically as shown in Table 1.3.

TABLE 1.3: THE CYBERNETIC HIERARCHY OF CONTROL

Function	*System*	*Controlling Subsystem*	*Interrelations*
Latency	Cultural System	Cultural Value	Informational
Integration	Social System	Collectivity	Controls
Goal-attainment	Personality System	Polity	↑ ↓
Adaptation	Organismic System	Economy	Energic Conditions

Thus, Parsons has emphasized the intra- and inter-systematic relationships of the four action systems. In his analysis, information is consistent with developing an idea of a cybernetic hierarchy of control. Parsons has applied this cybernetic hierarchy of control in the generalized media of exchange. Although Parsons has yet to describe the nature of these media clearly, he tries to link the basic types of media or information to the cybernetic hierarchy of control.

VII. SOCIAL CHANGE

Parsons's theory of social change is addressed through a chapter in *The Social System* entitled 'The Processes of Change of Social System' and his evolutionary social change model. Thus, Parsons deals with his theory of social change within the social systems, not a change of social systems (Turner, J., 1978: 486).

Parsons' social change can be explained through the concept of 'moving equilibrium'. However, Parsons does not think stable equilibrium is the most relevant concept for understanding society. This is because the social system is always in a 'moving' condition rather than stable. In this sense, his theory of social change has a dynamic aspect rather than purely static. Indeed, Johnson has argued that Parsons has always viewed social order as a problem to be explained, not to take for granted. Johnson makes a statement in Parsons's chapter on social change as follows: 'In other words, there is no such thing as equilibrated interaction; there is only a degree of approximation. Therefore, special processes are required to produce and maintain whatever approximations actually exist' (Jonshon, B. 1975: 35).

Moreover, Parsons says change is only possible if the vested interests bent on maintaining the system are overcome (Parsons, 1951: 496). Parsons (1961) recognizes both types of social change: exogenous and endogenous sources of structural change. Exogenous or external sources are changes in the environmental systems with which the social system interacts. Strains or imbalances are the internal sources of change. Strains result from the imperfect integration of various parts of the social system. On the personality system level, he states, 'the individual actor deals with elements of strain and conflict' using a 'mechanism of adjustment', such as withdrawal from interaction situations that cause strain or conflict (Wallace and Wolf, 1980: 37).

Parsons (1968) identifies several aspects of structural conflict. These are common problems in societal normative systems. Stratification is one of them. There are aspects of stratification that tend to promote conflict. In addition, regional, ethnic and religious differences tend to produce strains within a society. 'A pluralist society that incorporates variety must develop mechanisms to reduce the internal strains caused by the value differences' (Handel, 1993: 27-8).

Parsons distinguished between change in a system and change of a system. Handel expressed this distinction of Parsons as follows:

> Change in a system is produced by attempts to maintain equilibrium in response to strain. Sometimes, even specific institutions generate strain and change, such as science, which produces many technological changes. However, this sort of change is a natural part of social systems and usually does not involve changes in the most important values and may not affect the normative structure (ibid.: 28).

Parsons accepts that his theory of social change is 'fragmentary and incomplete' and concludes by saying, 'We do not in the present state of knowledge possess a general theory of the processes of change in societies as a whole' (Parsons, 1951: 534).

Thus, he does not make a specific and systematic clarification of the theory of social change and his approach is considered incomplete. However, strain is the central point of his analysis of the interactive system that leads to anxiety, phantasy, hostility or defense mechanisms. Still, he fails to specify under what circumstances and conditions strain will be developed.

VIII. EVOLUTIONARY MODEL

Parsons is interested in utilizing the action scheme and social change to analyse 'social evolution' across different historical periods, from simple to complex forms of society. Parsons's idea of social change is thoroughly examined in his work *Societies: Evolutionary and Comparative Perspectives.* In the evolutionary approach, he tries to make possible linkages between biological and societal evolution. Evolution, selection, adaptation, differentiation and integration are central to evolutionary theory and socio-cultural evolution, like organic evolution, is conceived as a movement from the simple to the complex forms of society. He argues that social evolution takes place due to changes in adaptation patterns. Haralambos put it, 'The history of human society from the simple hunting and gathering band to the complex nation-state represents an increase in the "general adaptive capacity" of society' (Haralambos, 1999: 529).

The intellectual foundations of Parsons' evolutionary model can be traced to several key thinkers and their societal development models. These include Comte's three stages of society—the theological, metaphysical, and scientific (or positivist) stages; Spencer's theory of societal evolution, which describes progress from simple to complex forms; Durkheim's distinction between mechanical and organic solidarity; Toennies' concept of *gemeinschaft* (community) and *gesellschaft* (society); and Marx's model of societal evolution from tribal society to a communist utopia. Parsons' evolutionary model, therefore, reflects a renewed interest in the evolutionary progression of human societies. Parsons proposes different elements involved in evolution based on Spencer's and Durkheim's understanding of societal development. These are:

1. Increasing differentiation of system units into patterns of functional interdependence;
2. Establishment of new principles and mechanisms of integration in differentiating systems; and

3. Increasing survival capacity of differentiated systems about the environment (Turner, J., 1978: 57).

From the perspective of action theory, evolution, therefore, involves (a) increasing differentiation of the personality, social, cultural and organismic systems from one another, (b) increasing differentiation within each of these four action subsystems, (c) escalating problems of integration and the emergence of new integrative structures, and (d) the upgrading of the survival capacity of each action subsystem, as well as of the overall action system, to its environment (Parsons, 1966).

Parsons identifies several evolutionary 'universals' in the discussion and elaboration of the basic model of evolution. He defines evolutionary 'universal' as 'any organizational development sufficiently important to further evolution that, rather than emerging only once, it is likely to be "hit upon" by various systems operating under different conditions' (Parsons, 1964: 339-57).

Parsons described,

> Six major evolutionary universals—social stratification, cultural legitimation, bureaucratic organization, money economy and market, generalized universalistic norms and democratic associations. This evolutionary sequence starts from and is made possible by greater differentiation and as societies develop and acquire these structures, they become still further differentiated (Wallace and Wolf, 1980: 40).

Parsons's evolutionary model incorporates structures and processes (Parsons, 1964: 10). The structures (patterned and stable relationships) are mainly the six evolutionary universals. In contrast, processes (evolutionary changes taking place in the system) are differentiation, adaptive upgrading, inclusion and value generalization.

In the evolutionary approach, Parsons maintained that four processes of social change are inevitable. The first, *differentiation*, refers to the increasing complexity of the social organization. The second evolutionary process is *adaptive upgrading*, whereby social institutions become more specialized in their purposes. It involves the idea of control or dominance of the environment. The third process identified by Parsons *is inclusion* (Parsons, 1966: 22).

Society must recognize that such factors have previously excluded groups like gender, race and social class background can contribute to the system's functioning.

Finally, Parsons contends that societies experience *value generation*, the development of new values that tolerate and legitimize a more excellent range of activities. In this context, Wallace points out, 'Higher levels of differentiation, adaptive upgrading and inclusion cannot coexist with a parochial value system that is shared by only a portion of the members of the social system' (Wallace and Wolf, 1980: 42).

All four processes identified by Parsons stress consensus are societal agreements on the nature of social organization and values.

Table 1.4 shows how each of these processes (the direction of all evolutionary processes is from differentiation to adaptive upgrading to inclusion to value generalization) has occurred in American society. Thus, for example, a change from 'medicine man' to physician, nurse, pharmacist and so forth is an illustration of differentiation in the field of medical science: the division of labour among physicians into obstetricians, internists, surgeons and so on illustrates adaptive upgrading in the field of health; a change in medical school enrolments from discriminating based on sex and race to opening their doors to Women and Blacks illustrates inclusion; and finally, a shift from a predominantly Protestant value system to American civil religion in the religious area is an example of value generalization.

TABLE 1.4: PARSONS' EVOLUTIONARY MODEL APPLIED TO PROCESSES IN THE UNITED STATES

Process:	Differentiation →	Adaptive upgrading →	Inclusion →	Value generalization
Examples	A change from medicine man to physician, nurse, pharmacist and so forth	The division of labour among physicians into obstetricians, internists, surgeons and so forth	To open the doors to various organizations for Women and Blacks	A change from Protestantism to civil religion

Parsons (1971) then outlines the pattern of evolution in different historical stages through the primitive, the intermediate and the modern. 'The intermediate differs from the primitive by the criterion of literacy; the modern, from the intermediate by the criterion of law. Each of the three stages has subdivisions or sublevels' (Bierstedt, 1981: 431).

Parsons distinguished primitive (aboriginal Australia) from 'advanced' primitive societies (African Kingdom). The intermediate stage is divided into the archaic, advanced or historic intermediate societies. The Indian subcontinent, China, Southeast Asia, the New World Societies of the Aztecs, Mayans, Incas, ancient Egypt and the Mesopotamian empires are examples of archaic societies. On the other hand, China and India (at different periods) and the Islamic and Roman Empires are examples of advanced intermediate societies.

The third stage in the evolution of societies is that of the modern social system. These societies evolved from the base of Western Christendom or the intermediate stage of evolution (also called the pre-industrial stage). Through the development of many social institutions, Western societies have succeeded in this process due to greater adaptive capacity, while others have failed. The United States is said to be 'the new lead society' and the 'leader of the modern system' (Parsons, 1971: 122).

Parsons's analysis of the evolution of societies can be represented in Table 1.5:

Bierstedt made some observations in connection with Parsons' evolutionary approach.

TABLE 1.5: EVOLUTION OF SOCIETIES

Primitive Societies		Intermediate Societies		Modern Societies
↓	↓	↓	↓	↓
Primitive Societies (Aboriginal Australia)	Advanced Primitive Societies (African Kingdom)	Archaic Societies (India, China, Southeast Asia, New World Societies)	Advanced Societies (China, India, Islamic and Roman Empire)	New Lead Society (USA)

First, Parsons's theoretical apparatus overwhelms his evolutionary account of transitioning from primitive via intermediate to modern societies. A second observation concerns the evolutionary theory itself. Although his awareness of socio-cultural evolution is not linear, he insists on this (Bierstedt, 1981: 433).

Throughout his work, Parsons was indebted to Emile Durkheim's analysis of societal progress from undifferentiated structures of primitive societies (characterized by mechanical solidarity) to structural differentiation in modern societies (characterized by organic solidarity). Both Durkheim and Parsons are very interested in dealing with the adjustment in the system rather than conflict, which leads them to establish the evolutionary model of society. However, neo-Parsonianism, neo-Marxism and neo-functionalism have criticized Parsonian theoretical orientation and tried to develop new theoretical views so that Parsons's analysis would be given a new direction.

IX. CONCLUSION

Talcott Parsons is considered the most outstanding American sociologist who has contributed significantly to the theories, methods, perspectives, approaches and concepts of sociology. In addition to his many thematic books, he has published six or seven volumes of essays dealing with a wide range of topics, from Christianity to psychoanalysis. Parsons accepted sociology as a scientific discipline and established a general and universal approach and theory in sociology. His conceptual schemes are more abstract and relatively free from the limitations of space and time.

Persons has adopted a functional approach to sociology. He deals with his functional approach regarding functional prerequisites such as *adaptation, goal-attainment*, *integration* and *latency*. In addition, Parsons emphasizes motivational orientation in his understanding of social action. He formulated *pattern variables* for theoretical analysis based on the logical method of classification of concepts. He considers a general and universally applicable theory in sociology that can be applied to any society at any period. This involves the understanding and analysis of the social system. However, in studying social change, he primarily discusses the evolutionary universals in various evolutionary stages of history. As a result, Parsons discovers a general theory of action with many systems, from studying personality systems to examining social systems and explaining cultural systems. This, indeed, covers the total gamut of social reality. Parsons distinguishes between changes in systems and in systems in the analysis of social change.

Parsons is not free from criticism. The first of these criticisms is that his system is essentially static; the actor never acts, approaches or attains the ends he seeks. Lewis Feuer says, 'Action in the Parsonian system tends to be translated into action' (Black, 1962: 155). Parsons's works are more related to static aspects than dynamics, systems in equilibrium rather than systems in conflict. Black and others have also noticed the conspicuous absence of causal propositions in Parsons's work. His pattern variables, system problems quadrilateral figures and tables are only classifications and have nothing to do with causal inquiry (Bierstedt, 1981: 436). Another criticism is that Parsons needs to pay more attention to strain, conflict and change. Instead, Parsons is only concerned with order and stability. In his sense, Parsons seems insensitive to his society's social and political issues.

Tom Bottomore (1969: 34-9) raises several issues on Parsonian analysis, including criticism. First, Bottomore criticizes that his theory is limited to conceptual schemes and does not consider empirical generalization. Secondly, he needs to include the logic or methodology of sociological inquiry in his conception of theory and discussion. Despite his various criticisms, Parsons was considered a leading figure in sociology in general and American sociology. However, Parsons provides a new direction in sociological concepts, theories and methods. Later, Parsonian functionalism was criticized by a new approach to sociology, i.e., neo-functionalism, in the 1980s by noted contemporary sociologist Jeffrey Alexander. However, Alexander also recognized Parsons's views on functionalism and tried to make some corrections to maintain the utility of the functional approach.

KEY TERMS

Action: A human behaviour in which four conditions are fulfilled is an action. These conditions are (i) attainment of ends or goals, (ii) it occurs in a situation, (iii) means, and (iv) normative values.

Archaic: Any society that is anticipated or old-fashioned.

Cathectic: Pertains to emotions such as affection, love, likeness and dislike.

Cognition: The process by which an individual comes to learn and interpre this environment. Cognition comprises all the methods by which an individual acquires knowledge, including perceiving, thinking, remembering, wondering, imagining, generalizing and judging.

Cultural System: A theoretical model of *culture* as a system of interrelated parts. Parsons has discussed it in the analysis of the social system. The cultural system is usually distinguished from the social system, referred to as the socio-cultural system.

Cybernetics: The study of communication among men, animals and machines, with particular emphasis on the *Feedback* of information and the function of Feedback in the process of control. Parsons deals with this concept in analysing the 'cybernetic hierarchy of control'.

Dichotomy: A *variable* having only two possible values. Sex is a dichotomous variable composed of two categories—male and female. Parsons deals with the notion of dichotomy in 'Pattern Variables'.

Diffuseness: The expectation in a social relationship is that the persons involved should have a wide range of rights and obligations. In a diffuse relationship, a wide range of personalities becomes engaged. For example, the roles of husbands, wives, fathers, mothers and friends are diffuse relations. Parsons discusses this concept in the 'diffuseness-specificity' type of *pattern variables.*

Evolutionary Universals: When social systems are viewed longer, some general directions of evolutionary developments are observed. The direction and nature of this historical process of evolution are called evolutionary universal.

Functional Requisite: A necessary condition for the survival of a *Social System.* The functional requisites of all societies include arrangements to provide for the biological necessities, provision for the socialization of the young, patterns of cooperation, etc.

Institutionalization: Institutionalization refers to predictable social behaviour, which is expected and considered legitimate in specific social roles. A system of sanctions is associated with institutionalization in terms of positive and negative sanctions.

Motivational Orientation: It refers to the mechanical aspects of action. This aspect of social action is separate from the values and norms of society.

Particularism: The orientation of an individual to another in terms of the unique nature of their relationship rather than abstract standards of behaviour. Parsons discusses it in the analysis of *Particularism-Universalism* pattern variables.

Pattern Variables: Parsons discussed the notion of pattern variables in terms of dilemmas or dichotomies between two variables involved in social relationships. According to Parsons, the five pattern variables represent a person's fundamental dilemmas in orienting others.

Self-orientation-Collective-orientation: This is one of the five pattern variables of Parsons. It refers to the opposition between personal and group interests in social situations. Parsons described it as the 'dilemma of private versus collective interests or the distribution between private permissiveness and collective obligation'.

Stress-Strain Concept: Parsons, in his functional approach, discusses that a social system is never in perfect equilibrium but always experiences inconsistencies among its parts, which produces stresses and strains.

Universalism: The orientation of a person to another person or persons in a situation in generalized standards of behaviour. Parsons has described it in 'Universalism-Particularism' variables. In some societies, universalism is a more widely expected pattern of behaviour than in others.

Universalism-Particularism: A pattern variable, a dichotomy in social behaviour which is concerned with the problem of whether a person in a given situation should be oriented to another person (or persons) in terms of generalized standard of behaviour or terms of the unique nature of their relationship to each other. This dichotomy or dilemma is one of the five *pattern variables* proposed by Talcott Parsons.

Utilitarian Approach: The ethical and social doctrine was established by Jermy Bentham. The sole aim and criterion for judging all human conduct and all laws is the amount of happiness produced for the most significant number of people.

Value Orientation: It refers to that orientation of social action governed by social norms and values, such as marrying someone within one's caste or class or wearing a formal dress for a formal party.

Voluntarism: In studying human behaviour, the orientation emphasizes individual choice and decision-making in determining behaviour. Thus, human behaviour is viewed as rational, purposive and not entirely determined by external forces.

REFERENCES

Abraham, M. Francis, *Modern Sociological Theory: An Introduction,* Oxford: Oxford University Press, 2000.

Bales, Robert Freed, *Interaction Process Analysis,* Cambridge, MA: Addison-Wesley, 1950.

Bierstedt, Robert, *American Sociological Theory: A Critical History,* London: Academic Press, 1981.

Black, 'Review of Social Theories of Talcott Parsons', *Journal of Philosophy,* 59, 29 March 1962.

Bottomore, Tom, 'Out of this World', *New York Review of Books,* 6 November 1969, pp. 34-9.

Coser, Lewis A., *Masters of Sociological Thought,* Jaipur: Rawat Publications, 1997.

Cuff, E.C., W.W. Sharrock and D.W. Francis, *Perspectives in Sociology,* London: Unwin Hyman, 1990.

Handel, Warren, H., *Contemporary Sociological Theory,* Englewood Cliffs: Prentice-Hall, Inc., 1993.

Haralambos, M., *Sociology: Themes and Perspectives,* Oxford: Oxford University Press, 1999.

Johnson, Benton, *Functionalism in Modern Sociology: Understanding Talcott Parsons,* Morristown: General Learning Press, 1975.

Loomis, Charles and Zona K. Loomis, *Modern Social Theories,* Princeton: D. Van Nostrand Company, 1965.

Parsons, Talcott. *The Social System.* England: London: Routledge, 1951.

——, 'An Outline of the Social System', in *Theories of Society,* edited by Talcott Parsons, Edward Shils, K.D. Naegele and J.R. Pitts, New York: Free Press, 1961.

——, 'Evolutionary Universals in Society', *American Sociological Review,* 29, 1964.

——, 'On Building Social System Theory: A Personal History', in *Social Systems and the Evolution of Action Theory,* New York: Free Press, 1977.

——, 'Some Comments on the State of the General Theory of Action', *American Sociological Review,* 18 December 1953: 618-31.

——, 'Social Interaction', pp. 429-41 in David Sills (ed.), *International Encyclopedia of the Social Sciences,* vol. 7, New York: Macmillan, 1968.

——, *Social System and the Evolution of Action Theory,* New York: Free Press, 1977.

——, *Societies: Evolutionary and Comparative Perspectives,* NJ: Englewood Cliffs: Prentice-Hall, Inc., 1966.

——, 'The Structure of Social Action', In *The Classical Tradition in Sociology: The American Tradition,* Volume II, edited by Jeffrey Alexander, Raymond Boudon and Mohamed Cherkaoni, London: Sage Publications, 1997.

——, *The Structure of Social Action,* New York: McGraw Hill Book Co.1937.

——, *The System of Modern Societies,* Englewood Cliffs: Prentice-Hall Inc., Prentice-Hall, 1971.

Parsons, Talcott and Edward A. Shills, *Toward a General Theory of Action,* Cambridge, MA: Harvard University Press, 1951a.

Shils, Edward A., Robert Freed Bales and Talcott Parsons, *Working Papers in the Theory of Action,* New York: Free Press, 1953.

Turner, Jonathan H., *The Structure of Sociological Theory,* Homewood: The Dorsey Press, 1978.

Wallace, Ruth A. and Alison Wolf, *Contemporary Sociological Theory: Continuing The Classical Tradition,* Englewood Cliffs: Prentice-Hall, Inc., 1980.

CHAPTER 2

Robert King Merton (1910-2003)

BIOGRAPHICAL SKETCH

Robert King Merton was an eminent American sociologist born on 5 July 1910 in the slums of South Philadelphia, Pennsylvania. His parents were immigrants from Eastern Europe. His father was a carpenter and truck driver. Merton grew up with a passion for knowledge and learning. At 8, he discovered the local public library and started reading various subjects. However, he was more interested in biography. He died on 23 February 2003.

In February 1927, Merton completed his graduation from the South Philadelphia High School for Boys. He got a scholarship at Temple University and immediately distinguished himself by the calibre of his academic year in the same year. He developed his interest in philosophy through his interaction with James Dunham, the dean of Temple University and a professor of philosophy. Later, he got inspiration in sociology from George E. Simpson, a young and enthusiastic instructor at this University.

In 1931, at twenty-one, Merton won a fellowship that took him to Harvard and graduated from sociology. At Harvard, Merton studied with a number of scholars. Some of them are Talcott Parsons, George Sarton, Pitrim Sorokin and L.J. Henderson. After that, Merton started to publish articles in various journals such as *Social Forces*, the *American Journal of Sociology*, the *American Sociological Review*, the *Quarterly Journal of Economics, Sociology and Social Research* and *Isis and the Scientific Monthly* (Bierstedt, 1981: 443).

In 1934, Merton became an instructor and tutor at Harvard and married Suzanne M. Carhart, a social worker who had also been a student at Temple University. He obtained a doctorate from Harvard University, where he was one of Parsons' earliest and most crucial graduate students. His doctorate work was published in *Osiris* in 1938 as *Science, Technology Society in Seventeenth-Century England.*

In 1939, he was appointed associate professor at Harvard University and, after that, professor at Tulane University. At Tulane University, he also worked as the chairman of the department. Two years later, in 1941, he accepted an appointment as assistant professor of sociology at Columbia University. In 1947, he became a professor at the same University and was named a Giddings professor in 1963. He also served as President of the American Sociological Association from 1956 to 1957 and the Eastern Sociological Society during 1968-9. He worked as an associate director of the University's Bureau of Applied Social Research from 1942 to 1971. Merton holds honorary degrees from Temple, Emory, Loyola (Chicago), Kalamazoo, Western Reserve, Chicago, Tulane, Colgate, Yale, Layden, Wales and Harvard. He holds the titles of extraordinary service professor and University Professor Emeritus.

At Harvard University, Merton was influenced by Pitrim Sorokin for theorizing, empirical research and statistical studies. At this time, he worked closely with another sociologist, Paul Lazarsfeld. Paul Lazarsfeld influenced Merton to become active in empirical research.

Merton, as a sociologist, was interested in a wide range of fields, including the sociology of science, the professions, sociological theory, and mass communication. He wrote extensively on topics such as science, housing, mass persuasion, interviews, business administration, and the student-physician. His work also covered subjects like social problems, Durkheim, Le Bon, Arabian intellectual development, invention, military techniques, civilization, population, time, sociology of knowledge, bureaucracy, personality, crime, the family, questionnaires, scale, radio and film propaganda, discrimination, public opinion polling, influence, research policy, epidemiology, friendship, medical schools, professions, corporations, quantification, genius, nursing, anomy, leadership and aging (Miles, 1975: 497-516). Despite his wide range of interests, Merton never produced a systematic theory or a comprehensive sociology book. *Social Theory and Social Structure* (1949) is considered Merton's significant contribution to sociology. In this book, he has written two classic essays on the relationship between sociological theory and empirical research, advocated a structural-functional approach to studying society and given the concepts of manifest and latent function and dysfunction. Besides functional analysis, he also discusses the concept of anomie and the theory of reference groups in this book. Other significant works in sociology are middle-range theory and his work on role sets. His other major publications are *Science, Technology and Society in Seventeenth-Century England* (1938), *Mass Persuasion* (1946), *On Theoretical Sociology* (1967), *Social Theory and Functional Analysis* (1969), and *The Sociology of Science* (1973).

I. SOCIOLOGICAL THEORIES OF THE MIDDLE-RANGE

Middle-range theories are abstract and are connected to empirical reality. They are involved in the research to clarify concepts, and a general theoretical orientation will be reformulated. In middle-range theories, 'the concepts and propositions of sociological theory will become more tightly organized as theoretically focused empirical research forces clarification, elaboration and reformulation of the ideas and propositions of each middle-range theory' (Turner, 1978: 70).

'Sociological Theories of the Middle-Range' is the second of the five essays in Merton's book *Social Theory and Social Structure.* Merton states in this book, 'Throughout this book, *sociological theory* refers to logically interconnected sets of propositions from which empirical uniformities can be derived' (Merton, 1957: 39).

In this way, Merton emphasized that theorists must invest their energies in constructing a limited number of theories based on research. Theorists must also consider 'consolidating the special theories into a more general set of concepts and mutually consistent propositions' (ibid.: 10).

Therefore, the unique theories of sociology must be formulated by concentrating on what they can after more general sociological theorizing. The theory of the middle-range will be discussed at any event. They are

> theories that lie between the minor but necessary working hypotheses that evolve in abundance during day-to-day research and the all-inclusive systematic efforts to develop a unified theory that will explain all the observed uniformities of social behaviour, social organization and social change (Merton, 1957: 39).

Thus, middle-range theories are involved in describing social phenomena. In Merton's view, middle-range theories provide a general theoretical orientation toward social phenomena.

The middle-range theory is used in sociology to guide empirical reality. The theory of reference group, the theory of relative deprivation and Merton's theory of the role set are examples of the use of middle-range theories. These theories are different from other sociological theories. Merton rightly points out about middle-range theory as follows:

> It is intermediate to general theories of social systems that are too remote from particular classes of social behaviour or organization and change to account for what is observed and those detailed orderly descriptions of particulars that are not generalized. The middle-range theory involves abstractions, of course, but they are close enough to observed data to be incorporated in propositions that permit empirical testing. Middle-range theories deal with delimited aspects of social phenomena (ibid.: 39).

Merton's theory of middle-range is primarily concerned with: (i) a guide to empirical inquiry, (ii) an intermediate between general and particular theories of the social system, (iii) abstractions that permit empirical testing, and (iv) delimited aspects of social phenomena.

The theory of the middle range is familiar and has well-established roots. This theory has been supported directly or indirectly by Bacon, Plato, Mill and some sociologists such as Hawkins, Ginsberg, Mannheim and Sorokin. Bacon emphasized the importance of 'middle axioms' in science as:

> The understanding must not, however, be allowed to jump and fly from particulars to remote axioms and of almost the highest generality (such as the

first principles, as they are called, of arts and things) and taking a stand upon them as truth that cannot be shaken, proceed to prove and frame the middle axioms by reference to them; which has been the practice hitherto; the understanding being not only carried that way by a natural impulse but also by the use of syllogistic demonstration trained and accustomed to it. But then and then only, may we hope well of the sciences, when in a just scale of ascent and by successive steps not interrupted or broken, we rise from particulars to lesser axioms and to middle axioms, one above the other and last of all to the most general. The lowest axioms differ slightly from bare experience, while the highest and most general (which we now have) are notional, abstract and without solidity. But the middle is the true and solid and living axioms, on which depend the affairs and fortunes of men; and above them, last, of all, those which are indeed the most general; such I mean as are not abstract, but of which those intermediate axioms are limitations (Bacon cites in Merton, 1957: 56).

John Stuart Mill and George Cornewall Lewis have supported Bacon's view on 'middle principles'. Lewis argues that limited theories involve predicting general tendencies and prevailing laws of causation by observing a restricted class of communities. On the other, Karl Mannheim, Adolf Lowe and Morris Ginsberg have discussed the concepts of *principia media, sociological middle principles*, and 'Mills treatment of middle principles in social science' respectively.

On the relevance of middle-range theory, Frank Hawkins concludes that:

Middle-range theories seem likely . . . to have greater explicative significance (than total sociological theories). Much has been done relating to mass communication, class stratification, bureaucracy, small groups of various types and other essential aspects of the social totality (Frank Hawkins cites in Merton, 1957: 58-9).

The middle-range theory has become necessary in sociology as far as empirical relevance is concerned. As Arthur K. Davis puts it, 'theories of the middle-range' in contrast to Parsons' more comprehensive approach, was well-conceived. . . . A middle-range focus-empirical analysis in a limited conceptual setting assures more securely the necessary continuous contact with empirical variables' (Davis cites in Merton, 1957: 59).

Peter H. Rossi, another advocator of empirical research, points out, 'the conception of "theories of the middle-range" gained widespread popularity among sociologists focused on empirical research as well as those concerned with theoretical development' (Rossi cites in Merton, 1957: 59).

In addition, Durkheim's monograph, *Suicide*, significantly contributes to the development of middle-range theory. To demonstrate Durkheim's approach to the 'middle-range' theory, Merton restated Durkheim's view in this way:

1. Social cohesion provides psychic support to group members subjected to acute stresses and anxieties.
2. Suicide rates are functions of unrelieved worries and stress to which persons are subjected.
3. Catholics have more significant social cohesion than Protestants.
4. Therefore, lower suicide rates should be anticipated among Catholics than among Protestants (ibid.: 151).

Merton takes his position on Durkheim's analysis of Suicide in middle-range theory because of empirical verification by further defining and operationalizing his concepts. Furthermore, Durkheim's study on suicide rates provides a background for Merton's theory of the middle range. In this sense, Durkheim hypothesized that anomie would lead to higher suicide rates. Merton, therefore, found that the Durkheimian concept of 'anomie' would help develop a theory of deviance. Merton concludes middle-range theory as follows:

1. Middle-range theories consist of limited assumptions from which empirical investigation logically derives and confirms.
2. These theories do not remain separate but are consolidated into wider networks of theory, as illustrated by theories of the level of aspiration, reference group and opportunity structure.
3. These theories are abstract and deal with different spheres of social behaviour and social structure to transcend sheer description or empirical generalization. The theory of social conflict

has been applied to ethnic and racial, class and international conflicts.

4. This type of theory is applicable in micro-sociological problems, as evidenced in small group research and macro-sociological difficulties, as evidenced in comparative studies of social mobility and formal organization and the interdependence of social institutions.
5. . . . many theories of the middle-range are consonant with a variety of systems of sociological thought.
6. Theories of the middle-range typically occur in a direct time of continuity with the work of classical theoretical formulations (Rossi cites in Merton, 1957: 68).

II. SOCIAL STRUCTURE AND ANOMIE

Merton's major work, *Social Structure and Anomie*, was published in 1938 as an article. Later, it is included in his book *Social Theory and Social Structure.* Merton's theory of 'anomie' is also known as the theory of deviance. The central aim of this theory is:

> What causes deviance, its rate and its type in a society? He expands Durkheim's concept of 'anomie' in his theoretical analysis. Unlike Durkheim, who emphasized man's overweening ambition to achieve unattainable goals, Merton sought to discover how *some social structures exert a definite pressure upon certain* persons in the society to engage in non-conforming rather than conforming conduct (Merton, 1957: 132).

Durkheim believes that anomie is the product of a lack of regulation. But, Merton emphasizes that anomie occurs due to discontinuity between cultural goals and the institutional means available to reach them. In this way, he first distinguishes social and artistic goals and the institutional norms to regulate them. Although every society has some norms that regulate individuals' social behaviour, they differ in how these norms are integrated with the hierarchy of values or cultural goals that appear to them. Deviant behaviour, therefore, occurred due to a lack of integration. Merton explains it, 'It is, indeed, my central hypothesis that aberrant behaviour may be regarded sociologically as a symptom of dissociation between culturally prescribed aspirations and socially structured avenues for realizing these aspirations' (Merton, 1957: 134).

Thus, Merton emphasizes that deviance or aberrant behaviour results from malintegration between institutionalized means and cultural goals.

Merton applies his analysis to the United States of America, where the goal of monetary success is heavily emphasized. Still, no corresponding emphasis is on the 'legitimate avenues to march toward this goal' (ibid.: 185-248). At this point, anomie results only in those groups who lack the means to attain goals. Turner rightly points out,

> the conditions under which institutionalized means are unequally available to the members of a social system. This situation is anomic for some population segments and sets into motion efforts to adapt or cope with the disjunction between means and ends. This disequilibrium causes deviance, with the rate and type of deviance reflecting the degree of disequilibrium or anomie and the location of affected populations in the social structure of a system (Turner, J., 1978: 85-6).

Merton discusses five possible ways in which members of American society can respond to success goals. He uses the 'plus (+)' and 'minus (–)' signs to classify five ways to explain 'anomie'. In this classification, Merton uses the (+) sign to indicate 'acceptance' of the goal of monetary success and the means to the goal. He uses the (–) sign to indicate 'rejection' of the goal or means. Merton's classification of five ways is conformity, innovation, ritualism, retreatism and rebellion. His analysis of deviant behaviour or anomie can be presented as shown in Table 2.1.

TABLE 2.1: TYPOLOGY OF ADAPTATIONS TO ANOMIE

	Modes of Adaptation	*Cultural Goals*	*Institutionalized Means*
I.	Conformity	+	+
II.	Innovation	+	–
III.	Ritualism	–	+
IV.	Retreatism	–	–
V.	Rebellion	±	±

I. *Conformity:* It is not a type of deviance but is widely diffused and the most common type of adaptation. The individual uses institutionalized means to achieve cultural goals. As Turner puts it,

> the more widespread and psychologically salient are culturally defined success goals and the more equally available to members of the system are culturally legitimated structural means for realizing them, the less the potential for anomie and the higher the rates of conforming behaviour in that system (Turner, J., 1978: 88).

The other four types of adaptation are considered to be deviant.

II. *Innovation:* It is a social mode of adaptation. Innovation occurs when an individual accepts the goals but rejects the institutional norms governing the means for their attainment. Merton explains it,

> It is only when a system of cultural values extols, virtually above all else, certain *common success goals for the population at large* while the social structure rigorously restricts or completely closes access to approved modes of reaching these goals for a *considerable part of the same population*, that deviant behaviour ensues on a large scale (Merton, 1957: 146).

Merton argues that members of the lower sections of society are most likely to select this route to success. Robbery, theft, embezzlement, forgery and cheating at the examination are examples of innovation. Turner explains it in the form of a proposition,

> The less available to members of a population are culturally legitimated structural means and the fewer internal prohibitions against the use of culturally non-legitimated means, the greater the incidence of innovative behaviour in that population, when: (a) cultural values dictating individual achievement are widespread and salient, and (b) illegitimate means are more readily available (Turner, J., 1978: 88).

In innovative types of deviance, poverty and crime are interlinked.

III. *Ritualism:* Ritualism is the third type of mode of adaptation. 'Status anxiety' is central to ritualism. Merton argues that 'status anxiety' is experienced by those who have some degree of access to means but experience acute anxiety while using means for competitive efforts at success. In ritualism, individuals resolve their status-anxiety by conforming to means and rejecting the success goals. This type of deviant behaviour is found among the lower middle class. However, in comparison to working-class members, the lower-middle-class members have been strongly socialized to conform to social norms and hence are away from committing a crime. Turner explains it,

> The greater the availability of culturally legitimated structural means to members of a population and the greater the status anxiety experienced by members of this population in the pursuit of cultural success goals, the greater the incidence of ritualistic behaviour among that population, when: (a) cultural values dictating individual achievement are widespread and salient, and (b) socialization experiences create strong psychological commitments to culturally legitimated means (Turner, J., 1978: 89).

The ritualist, therefore, is deviant because the person has rejected the success goals held by most members of society.

IV. *Retreatism:* According to Merton, the fourth mode of adaptation is retreatism. In retreatism, an individual has strongly internalized cultural goals and the institutionalized means to achieve success. They resolve the conflict of their situation by abandoning both the goals and the means of reaching them. In the words of Turner,

> The less available to members of a population are culturally legitimated structural means and the greater the internal prohibitions against the use of culturally illegitimate means, the greater the incidence of retreats behaviour in that population, when: (a) cultural values dictating individual achievement are widespread and salient, and (b) socialization experiences create strong commitments to culturally legitimate means (ibid.).

Retreatism is found among psychotics, autists, pariahs, outcasts, vagrants, vagabonds, tramps, chronic drunkards and drug addicts.

V. *Rebellion:* The fourth and last mode of adaptation is rebellion. It is based on rejecting cultural goals and the institutionalized means and their replacement by different goals and means. As Turner puts it,

> The more the members of a population experience a sense of frustration and deprivation over their involvement in culturally legitimated structural means

for realizing success goals and the more available to these members are groupings which ideologically criticize the structure of the system, the greater the incidence of rebellions behaviour in that population (Turner, J., 1978: 90).

Merton argues that: 'it is typically members of a rising class rather than the most depressed strata who organize the resentful and rebellious into a revolutionary group' (Merton cites in Haralambos, 1999: 415).

In this sense, organized political action, populist movements and revolutionary upheavals are examples of rebellion.

Having discussed the typology of modes of adaptation, Merton defines anomie as:

A breakdown in the cultural structure occurring particularly when there is an acute disjunction between the cultural norms and goals and the socially structured capacities of members of the group to act in accord with them. In this conception, cultural values may help produce behaviour at odds with the mandates of the values themselves (Merton, 1957: 162).

In other words, Merton claims that society's culture and structure generate deviance. The condition of anomie occurs when the maladjustment between the social structure and the cultural values occurs. In addition, Merton also distinguishes between two types of anomie: 'simple' and 'acute' anomie. In the words of Merton:

Simple anomie refers to the state of confusion in a group of society that is subject to conflict between value systems, resulting in some degree of uneasiness and a sense of separation from the group; acute anomie to the deterioration and, at the extreme, the disintegration of value-systems, which results in marked anxieties (ibid.: 217).

In short, Merton accepts that the conflict between cultural goals and institutionalized means is the primary source of anomie. However, he also emphasizes that anomie is a sociological concept rather than a psychological one.

Anomie, then, is a condition of the social surround, not a condition of particular people. People are *confronted* by substantial anomie when, as a matter of objective fact, they cannot rely upon a high probability that the behaviour of others will be in rough accord with standards *jointly* regarded as legitimate (Merton cites in Abraham, 2000: 183).

This statement makes Merton a sociologist. This theory can be applied to any society, not only 'the existing society'. However, Merton is modest in his claims that all kinds of deviance, such as crime and juvenile delinquency, can be explained by a single theory of anomie.

Furthermore, he does not claim that all deviance is criminal. For instance, illness and genius may be considered deviant, although they do not violate society's norms. Finally, let us consider Merton's last word on this subject:

> Since it is so easily forgotten, it should also be said that to central this theory upon the cultural and structural sources of deviant behaviour is not to imply that such behaviour is the characteristic, let alone the exclusive, response to the pressures we have been examining. This is an analysis of varying *rates* and *types* of deviant behaviour, not an empirical generalization that all those subject to these pressures responds by deviation. The theory only holds that those located in places in the social structure that are particularly exposed to such stresses are more likely to exhibit deviant behaviour. Yet, as a result of countervailing social mechanisms, most stressful positions do not *typically* induce deviation; conformity tends to remain the model response (Merton, 1957: 183).

In brief, Merton presents an innovative sociological theory of deviance. He argues that deviance is a result of society's nature rather than the individual's. Furthermore, two of his five categories—innovation and rebellion, are concerned with social change. Merton's theory of anomie is considered one of the significant contributions to sociology.

III. FUNCTIONAL ANALYSIS

Parsons and Merton prefer to use the word *functional analysis* rather than *structural-functionalism.* Merton attempts to refine and develop a functional approach. His primary aim in functional analysis is to trace the significant errors in structural functionalism. Combining the outlined criticisms of functional structuralism and empirical studies in functional analysis is necessary for a research strategy. As Handel puts it,

> The criticisms and the research strategy are inseparable because the strategy is designed specifically to eliminate the substantive assumptions of the structural functionalists and to substitute more rigorous empirical studies of functional connections (Handel, 1993: 39).

In this context, Merton first introduced new terminology. But, then, Merton rightly points out terminological confusion: 'Too often, a single term has been used to symbolize different concepts, just as different terms have symbolized the same concept' (Merton, 1957: 74).

Merton begins his functional analysis with definitional problems of the word *function* burdened with different connotations. Nevertheless, various words express the same connotation, including use, utility, purpose, motive, intention, aim and *consequences.* After that, Merton goes on to establish three postulates in functional theory. Merton has explained:

> Substantially, these postulates hold. First, standardized social activities or cultural items are functional for the entire social or cultural system; second, all social and cultural items fulfil sociological functions; and third, these items are consequently *indispensable* (ibid.: 79).

Merton establishes three prevailing postulates in functional analysis to point out the distinctive difficulties of structural functionalism. These are:

(i) *The Postulate of the Functional Unity of Society:* This postulate assumes that any particular element of society, functional, must be functional to maintain the *whole* society. In this context, Merton cites some noted sociologists and anthropologists, such as Radcliff Brown, Malinowski, Kluckohn, Parker, Davis and Moore. They discussed small-scale societies, and this assumption is valid only for such types of societies. Therefore, the functional unity of society is doubtful, argues Merton, particularly for complex and highly differentiated societies. For instance, it would be wrong to consider that religious ceremonial promoted solidarity throughout Indian society. Still, it would be accurate to say that it contributes to the solidarity of subgroups within it. Here Merton says,

This unity of the whole society cannot be usefully posited before observation. It is a question of fact and not a matter of opinion. The theoretical framework of functional analysis must expressly require *specification* of the *units* for which a given social or cultural item is functional. It must explicitly allow for a given item having diverse consequences, functional and dysfunctional, for individuals, for subgroups and the more inclusive social structure and culture (Merton, 1957: 84).

Merton contends that functional unity is a matter of observation and investigation. Functional unity applies only to a small type of society in which a change in one part of the system will automatically change other parts. He suggests that a high degree of 'functional autonomy' is found in highly differentiated societies, not functional unity.

(ii) *The Postulate of Universal Functionalism:* This postulate states that 'all standardized social or cultural forms have positive functions' (ibid.). For instance, nineteenth-century anthropo-logists such as Malinowski, Kluckhohn, Rivers, Tylor, Durkheim assumed that every social and cultural pattern must have positive functions for the maintenance of society. But the fact is that not every structure, custom, belief and so forth has positive functions. He suggests that functionalists should analyse any part of society to keep their mind from functional, dysfunctional or nonfunctional. According to Merton, functionalists should clearly explain any particular unit of society in terms of functional, dysfunctional or nonfunctional. These units may be individuals, groups or society as a whole. For instance, poverty may not be dysfunctional for society as only for the poor. Merton recommends that the postulate of universal functionalism is to be replaced by:

the provisional assumption that persisting cultural forms have a *net balance of functional consequences* either for the society considered as a unit or for sub-groups sufficiently powerful to retain these forms intact, using direct coercion or indirect persuasion (ibid.: 86).

(iii) *Postulates of Indispensability:* According to Merton, the last and third postulate of functional analysis is the postulate of indispensability. This postulate states that some institutions or social arrangements are indispensable to society. This postulate is related to two assertions.

First, it is assumed that certain functions are indispensable in the sense that, unless they are performed, the society (or group or individual) will not persist. This, then, sets forth a concept of functional prerequisites or preconditions functionally necessary for a society . . . Second, . . . it is assumed that *certain cultural or social forms* are indispensable for fulfilling each of these functions' (Merton, 1957: 87).

Merton raises questions on the assumption of indispensability and rejects it by arguing that: 'just as the same item may have multiple functions, so may alternative items diversely fulfill the same function' (ibid.: 87-8).

Merton suggests the concept of functional alternatives, functional equivalents or functional substitutes to replace the idea of indispensability. This concept is widely recognized and used in every discipline of functional analysis. Moreover, functional alternatives could have some equivalent consequences within a given system.

The utility of this concept is not to identify various arrangements with identical consequences, but rather to identify arrangements with identical or similar functions (effectiveness) but reduced dysfunctions (increased efficiency) (Handel, 1993: 40).

Merton, therefore, accepts that specific functions must be met for society by a range of alternative means rather than the institutions that meet them, which are indispensable to survival.

In a nutshell, these postulates are debatable and unnecessary. Nevertheless, these are the codifications of the mode of functional analysis. In *the postulate of functional unity*, Merton accepts the impossibility of full integration of all societies and argues that it should be analysed by finding a range of degrees of integration based on the specification of social units subserved by given social functions. Thus, a functional analysis should identify which institutions hurt groups and which groups are helped. The second postulate of *universal functionalism* is based on the assumption that *every standardized social or cultural form is functional.*

In contrast, Merton argues that some arrangements may have developed to fill some function but have survived with current functions. The third postulate of *indispensability* is based on the assumption that *certain functions must be accomplished if a society is to survive and that the institutions that fulfil these functions are indispensable.* Merton has given the concept of *functional necessity or functional prerequisites and functional alternatives, equivalents or substitutes* to counter these postulates.

Merton's position on these functional postulates relies on nonempirical assertions based on abstract, theoretical systems. However, he emphasized that functionalists should examine the situation empirically. Merton's belief that empirical tests are crucial to a functional analysis led him to develop his 'paradigm' of functional analysis as a guide to integrating theory and research.

A PARADIGM FOR FUNCTIONAL ANALYSIS IN SOCIOLOGY

Merton, in this section, is concerned with dealing with the necessity of a paradigm that contains a set of concepts without which the sociologist cannot adequately carry out a functional analysis. As Merton puts it,

> The paradigm brings these (*concepts, postulates, vocabularies* and *ideological imputations*) together in compact form, thus permitting simultaneous inspection of the major requirements of functional analysis and serving an aid to self-correction of provisional interpretations. . . . The paradigm presents the core of concepts, procedures and inference in functional analysis (Merton, 1957: 104).

Merton sets out a long and complicated paradigm, including concepts and queries, containing eleven rubrics or headings:

1. *The item(s) to which functions are imputed:* Merton clarifies that functional analysis focuses on groups or organizations, societies and cultures. He stated that any object subjected to functional analysis must:

> represent a *standardized* (i.e., patterned and repetitive) item. These items are, according to Merton, social roles, institutional patterns, social processes, cultural patterns, culturally patterned emotions, social norms, group organizations, social structures, devices for social control, etc. (ibid.).

In addition, Merton argues that analysis of sociological data is necessary for functional analysis.

2. *Concepts of subjective dispositions (motives, purposes):* Functional analysis involves the merger of subjective disposition concepts, such as motives and purposes of the individual, with the concepts of objective consequences of attitude, belief and behaviour. In a social system, the subjective disposition of the individual is not to be confused with the concepts of objective consequences.

3. *Concepts of objective consequences (functions, dysfunctions):* The focus of the functionalist should be on social functions rather than individual motives. Merton, here, attempts to eliminate conceptual confusion involved in functional analysis. He defined and distinguished the concepts of functions, dysfunctions, latent and manifest functions as follows:

> Functions are those observed consequences that make for the adaptation or adjustment of a given system and dysfunctions are those observed consequences that lessen the system's adaptation or adjustment. There is also an empirical possibility of *nonfunctional* implications, which are irrelevant to the system under consideration.
>
> In any given instance, an item may have functional and dysfunctional consequences, giving rise to the complicated and important problem of solving canons for assessing the net balance of the aggregate of implications.
>
> The second problem (arising from the easy confusion of motives and functions) requires us to introduce a conceptual distinction between the cases in which the subjective aim-in-view coincides with the objective consequences and how they diverge.
>
> *Manifest functions* are those objective consequences contributing to the system's adjustment or adaptation, which are intended and recognized by participants.
>
> *Latent functions,* correctively, are those which are neither intended nor recognized (Merton, 1957: 105).

4. *Concepts of the unit subserved by the function:* Merton points out that every item may be dysfunctional or functional for society as a whole but for a particular section. In other words, some items may be functional for one group and dysfunctional for another group or subsystem.

5. *Concepts of functional requirements (needs, prerequisites):* The assumption of functional requirements involves re-examining fulfilling conditions of 'survival' or meeting the system's 'biological needs'. 'This involves the difficult problem of establishing *types* of functional requirements (universal *vs* specific); procedures for validating the assumption of these requirements; etc.' (Merton, 1957: 106).

6. *Concepts of the mechanisms through which functions are fulfilled:* Functional analysis must seek to identify and analyse the social mechanisms through which functions are fulfilled (Abraham, 2000: 84).

7. *Concepts of functional alternatives (functional equivalents or substitutes):* Merton abandoned the gratuitous assumption of the functional indispensability of particular social structures. Instead, they emphasized the requirement of some concepts, such as functional alternatives, equivalents or substitutes. In this sense,

> we must focus on the range of possible variation in the items which can serve as functional alternatives, equivalents or substitutes (ibid.: 85).

8. *Concepts of structural context (or structural constraint):* Functional analysis must recognize the interdependence of the elements of the social structure and the limited range of variation in the items that can fulfil designated functions in the social system. As Merton puts it,

> Failure to recognize the relevance of interdependence and attendant structural constraints leads to utopian thought in which it is tacitly assumed that certain elements of a social system can be eliminated without affecting the rest of that system (Merton, 1957: 107).

9. *Concepts of dynamics and change:* Functional analysts generally focus on social structure statics and neglect the study of structural change (ibid.). Merton accepts the role of dys-function in social change. He writes:

> The concept of dysfunction, which implies the idea of strain, stress and tension on the structural level, provides an analytical approach to the study of dynamics and change (ibid.).

10. *Problems of validation of functional analysis*: Merton emphasizes validating various functional assumptions, postulates, imputations and observations.

> This requires a rigorous statement of the sociological procedures of analysis which most nearly approximate the *logic* of experimentation. Moreover, it requires a systematic review of the possibilities and limitations of the *comparative* (cross-cultural and cross-group) *analysis* (Merton, 1957: 108).

11. *Problems of the ideological implications of functional analysis*: Have no intrinsic commitment to any ideological position.

Having discussed the paradigm for functional analysis, Merton describes the *purposes* and *utilities* of paradigm in sociological analysis in five ways (Merton in Alexander et al., 1997: 333-48):

(*i*) Firstly, paradigms provide a notational function. 'They provide a compact parsimonious arrangement of the central concepts and their interrelations as these are utilized for description and analysis . . .' (ibid.: 345).

(*ii*) Secondly, the paradigm provides a pragmatic and logical guide for avoiding *ad hoc* (i.e., logically irresponsible) hypotheses.

(*iii*) The third purpose of the paradigm is to advance the *cumulation* of theoretical interpretation. In this connection, the paradigm provides a foundation upon which the house of theoretical understandings is built.

(*iv*) The fourth purpose is to systematically cross-tabulate significant concepts and sensitize the sociologist toward empirical and theoretical problems.

(*v*) The fifth and final purpose of the paradigm is to codify qualitative analysis methods logically.

Merton provides a new direction to functional analysis by giving three postulates to explain the functional approach and provides a detailed analysis of the paradigm to remove conceptual confusion. Merton applies it in different aspects of various types of society.

IV. BEARING OF SOCIOLOGICAL THEORY ON EMPIRICAL RESEARCH

Merton analysed the relations of sociological theory and empirical research in his major work, *Social Theory and Social Structure,* in the form of an article entitled 'Bearing of Sociological Theory on Empirical Research'. Sociological theory refers 'to the products of several related, but distinct activities carried on by members of a professional group called sociologists' (Merton, 1957: 140).

Merton discussed six types of work essential to make the relationship between sociological theory and empirical research—(1) methodology; (2) general sociological orientations; (3) analysis of sociological concepts; (4) *post factum* sociological interpretations; (5) empirical generalizations in sociology; and (6) sociological theory.

1. *Methodology:* Merton believes that sociologists must be methodologically wise and aware of the design of the investigation, the nature of inference and the requirements of a theoretical system (ibid.: 140-1).

   The methodology is free of sociological problems. In this sense, sociologists must make a clear 'difference between *knowing how to test* a battery of hypotheses and *knowing the theory* from which to derive hypotheses to be tested' (ibid.: 141).

   An appropriate methodological approach would be fruitful in bridging methodological aspiration and actual sociological attainment.
2. *General sociological orientations:* The textbook describes much of a sociological theory of general orientations toward sub-stantive materials. 'Such orientations involve broad postulates that indicate types of variables that are somehow taken into account rather than specifying determinate relationships between particular variables' (ibid.: 141-2).

   These general orientations provide a broader framework for empirical inquiry. Sociologists have 'to detect sociological gaps in applying their theory to concrete social behaviour' (ibid.: 143).

3. *Analysis of sociological concepts:* Conceptual analysis is a crucial phase in theoretical orientation. 'Concepts, then, constitute the definitions (or prescriptions) of what is to be observed; they are the variables between which empirical relationships are to be sought. When propositions are logically interrelated, a theory has been instituted' (Merton, 1957: 143).

   Thus, selecting concepts is a crucial part of empirical inquiry.
4. Post factum *sociological interpretations: Post factums* are designed to 'explain' observations. Such '*post factum* explanations' differ in logical function from speciously similar procedures where the observational materials are utilized to *derive* fresh hypotheses from being confirmed by *new* observations (ibid.: 147).

   Post factum explanation remains at the level of *plausibility* (low evidential value) rather than leading to 'compelling evidence' (a high degree of confirmation). (Merton, 1957: 147).

   Plausibility is found only when an interpretation is consistent with one set of data. On the other, 'the absence of compelling evidence stems from the failure to provide specific tests of the interpretations apart from their consistency with the initial observations (ibid.: 148).
5. *Empirical generalizations in sociology:* Empirical generalizations in sociology involve all isolated propositions summarizing observed uniformities of relationships between two or more variables. Empirical inquiry is engaged in the process of direct research. If an empirical investigation is organized and empirical uniformities are discovered, then there is a possibility of developing a theoretical system.
6. *Sociological theory:* To make the relationship between empirical generalization and sociological theory, it may be helpful to examine a typical case in which such empirical generalizations were incorporated into a body of substantive theory.

Merton, in a nutshell, points out the facts necessary to make relations between sociological theory and empirical research. In his own words,

1. Once having established the theoretic pertinence of uniformity by deriving it from a set of interrelated propositions, we provide for the *cumulation* of both theory and research findings.
2. Converting empirical uniformities into theoretic statements thus increases the *fruitfulness* of research through the successive exploration of implications.
3. By providing a rationale, the theory introduces a *ground for prediction* that is more secure than mere empirical extrapolation from previously observed trends.
4. If a theory is to be productive, it must be sufficiently *precise* to be *determinate.* Hence, precision is an integral element of the criterion of *testability.*
5. . . . precise predictions and data reduce the *empirical* bearing upon the research of the *logical* fallacy of affirming the consequent (Merton, 1957: 151-2).

In the analysis of the two, there are few instances to formulate hypotheses derived from a given theory. Hypotheses, according to Merton, could be prepared with the help of empirical inquiries rather than central theoretic orientation. The bulk of general directions and conceptual analyses reflect the tendency to separate theoretical activity from empirical research. 'It is commonplace that continuity, rather than dispersion, can be achieved only if empirical studies are theory-oriented and if a theory is empirically confirmable' (ibid.: 154).

The correlative process between sociological theory and empirical research is termed 'codification'. The term 'codification' is given by Lazarsfeld. Formal derivation focuses on the implications of a theory, whereas codification seeks to systematize available empirical generalizations in *apparently different* spheres of behaviour. In this context, codification creates theoretical problems. 'A codified for-mulation, even as crude as this, gives rise to theoretic problems which would be readily overlooked if the several empirical findings were not re-examined within a single context' (ibid.: 155).

Hence, codification facilitates the co-development of viable sociological theory and pertinent empirical research.

V. REFERENCE GROUP THEORY

Reference group theory is one of the significant contributions of Merton to sociological theory. This theory appears in the long papers, the first of which, written in collaboration with Alice S. Rossi, deals with the theory itself and the second with continuities. The concept 'relative deprivation', given in *The American Soldier* by Samuel A. Stouffer, is central to reference group theory. Relative deprivation is utilized to interpret variations in attitudes among different categories of men concerning age, education, marital status, etc. To discuss the relationship between the concept of relative deprivation with reference group theory, it is essential to relate them with the notion of 'others' that represent non-membership or out-groups. A series of concepts, such as membership and non-membership groups, out- and in-groups, are involved in this sense. As Merton says, 'Reference groups are, in principle, almost innumerable; any of the groups of which one is a member and these are, of course, can become points of reference for shaping one's attitudes, evaluating and behaviour' (Merton, 1957: 233).

The critical focus of inquiry in reference group theory is that people orient their attitude and behaviour toward the other group members to which they do not belong.

The main aim of reference group theory is 'to systematize the determinants and consequences of those processes of evaluation and self-appraisal in which the individual takes the values or standards of other individuals and groups as a comparative frame of reference' (Merton cites in Alexander et al., 1997: 137).

The precise nature of the theory of the reference group can be better seen through a detailed conceptual analysis.

Relative Deprivation: In developing the concept of relative deprivation, the authors of *The American Soldier,* on the whole, centred their attention on the deprivation component rather than the comparative component. This concept is primarily used to understand soldiers' dissatisfaction, deprivation or injustice. Authors recognize that:

> 'deprivation' is the incidental and particularised component of relative deprivation, whereas the more significant nucleus of the concept is its stress upon

social and psychological experience as 'relative'. . . . It is the *relative* component, the standards of comparison in self-evaluation, that these concepts have in common (Merton cites in Alexander et al., 1997: 138).

The concept of relative deprivation makes a ground for reference group behaviour.

The Concept of Group and Group Membership: The concept of group and its various typologies are involved in studying a reference group. Merton expressed three ways to understand group and group memberships:

(*i*) *Sociological concept of a group:* It refers to several people interacting with one another under established patterns (Merton, 1957: 339). Here, people are involved in the process of social interaction. This is only known as the *objective* criterion of the group based on the *frequency of interaction.*

(*ii*) A group's second criterion is that the interacting persons *define themselves* as 'members' (ibid.: 340). At this point, their interaction is morally binding on all the group members.

(*iii*) The correlative and third criterion is that others define the persons in interaction as 'belonging to the group' (ibid.: 340). These others include fellow members and non-members.

In this context, it is necessary to distinguish social groups from *social categories* and *collectivities.* Social categories refer 'to established statuses between the occupants of which there may be little or no interaction' (ibid.: footnotes, 287). On the other, all groups are collectivities, but all collectivities are not groups. Therefore, the collectivities that lack involvement in the interaction among members are not groups.

The Concept of Non-Membership: Merton accepts that men and women try to stay in their group. But 'they frequently orient themselves to groups other than their own in shaping their behaviour and evaluations'. Thus, Merton defines 'non-members are those who do not meet the interactional and definitional criteria of membership' (ibid.: 342).

Non-members have always tended to become members of another group. However, they differ in their attitudes toward becoming members. Merton analyses three ways to become member of a group:

> (a) some may aspire to membership in the group; (b) others may be indifferent toward such affiliation; and (c) still others may be motivated to remain unaffiliated with the group. Reference group theory has, of course, incorporated the first of these motivated attitudes toward membership as constituting one mechanism making for positive orientation of non-members toward the norms of a group (Merton, 1957: 343).

However, for reference groups, an individual adopts the values and norms of a group to which he aspires but does not belong.

The concepts of in-group and out-group: William Graham Sumner first introduced the concepts of in-group and out-group. In the words of Sumner, '. . . a differentiation arises between ourselves, the we-group or in-group and everybody else or the other-groups, out-groups' (Sumner cites in Merton, 1957: 351).

It is a fact that membership groups are not co-terminus within-groups, nor non-membership groups with out-groups. Reference group theory treats both types of groups.

Positive and negative reference groups: Reference groups, as outlined by Merton, are of two types. A positive reference group is synonymous with a reference group. In contrast, a negative reference group is whose norms and activities an individual uses to guide what he shall reject and oppose. Merton defines, in his own words.

> The positive type involves motivated assimilation of the norms of the group or the standards of the group as a basis for self-appraisal; the negative type involves motivated rejection, i.e., not merely non-acceptance of norms but the formation of counter-norms (Merton, 1957: 354).

The concept of anticipatory socialization: The consequence of conforming to the norms of a group other than one's own is discussed in the concept of *anticipatory socialization.* It means that 'individuals begin to conform to the norms of the groups to which they want to belong in preference to the norms of the groups to which they wish to belong in preference to the norms of the groups to which they belong' (Bierstedt, 1981: 472).

Merton talks about anticipatory socialization in the context of non-membership reference groups. In anticipatory socialization, only vertical mobility is possible. Anticipatory socialization can be seen through different career patterns: a life-medical student into a doctor, a graduate student into a lecturer, a lawyer into a law firm partner, a recruit into a member of the team, a clerk into a supervisor, etc.

Merton and Rossi further argue that although anticipatory socialization may be functional for the individual, it can be dysfunctional for the group. For instance, conformity rewards individuals and helps sustain authority in the group and larger social systems.

The preceding discussion of relative deprivation, group, membership and non-membership, in- and out-groups, collectivities and social categories, positive and negative reference groups and anticipatory socialization is oriented to understanding the reference group theory. To understand reference group theory, it is essential to discuss the determinants and structural elements of reference groups.

DETERMINANTS OF REFERENCE GROUP

Merton emphasizes the determining factors that one chooses as reference groups. Merton speaks of three possibilities in which an individual takes other individuals' or groups' values or standards as a comparative frame of reference. These are reference individuals, selection among different membership groups and the selection of non-membership groups. Finally, Merton elaborates on the determinants that stimulate the same individual to choose other reference groups for various purposes.

1. *Hyman originally introduced the selection of Reference Groups and Reference Individuals*: The term includes behaviour oriented to groups and particular individuals. The individuals are interested in selecting not only reference groups but they choose reference individuals also. The reference individual here is similar to a *role model.* An individual usually has more than one role, such as charisma, status, etc. The role model concept can be

considered more restricted in scope, denoting a more limited identification with an individual in only one or a few selected roles (Merton, 1957: 356-7). But the person who identifies with a reference individual will seek to 'approximate the behaviour and values of that individual in his several roles'. Merton accepts biographers, editors of 'Fan magazines' and 'gossip columnists' as reference individuals.

2. *Selection of Reference Groups among Non-membership Groups:* Merton is fascinated by non-membership groups. At the same time, he warns that the groups probably influence more people. However, he emphasized why and under what circumstances men choose non-membership groups as their reference groups. According to Merton, three factors are involved in selecting non-membership groups. First, 'the selection of reference groups is primarily governed by the capacity of certain groups to *confer some prestige in terms of the institutional structure of the society* (ibid.: 359). In this context, power and status are the primary basis for selecting non-membership groups.

Second, it examines what kind of people generally accept non-membership groups as reference groups. Merton answers it is typically the 'isolates' in a group who may be particularly ready to adopt the values of non-membership groups as normative frames of reference (ibid.: 359).

The 'isolates', who are supposed to be sensitive and rebellious, are more intense in mobility toward other groups to which they do not belong.

Third, it suggests that 'social systems with relatively high rates of social mobility will tend to make for widespread orientation to non-membership groups as reference groups' (ibid.: 359).

This factor applies to the people of an open system in which anticipatory socialization will function.

3. *The Selection of Reference Groups among Membership Groups:* Merton points out a general tendency among people to influence their groups. But the fact is 'that non-membership groups constitute the *exclusive* focus for reference group theory' (ibid.: 361).

A person may belong to innumerable groups, from family to religious groups. Membership groups are mainly based on two frames of reference, i.e., normative and comparative. Normative is permanent, whereas comparative is temporary. A membership group that will not last long is unlikely to be chosen as a reference group and is considered temporary. For instance, a class of undergraduate students lasts only three years and is deemed quick. On the other hand, a group, such as a kinship, a caste group or a professional group, stays for a long time as a reference group and is considered *permanent.*

STRUCTURAL ELEMENTS OF REFERENCE GROUPS

The structural elements are centrally involved in reference group behaviour conceived as a social process. In this context, *observability* or *visibility* plays a significant role in this process.

1. *Observability and Visibility: Patterned Avenues of Information about Norms, Values and Role-performance:* Reference group theory assumes that individuals who compare their lot with others have some knowledge of the situation in which these others find themselves (Merton, 1957: 390). In other words, as Merton outlines, the theory of reference group behaviour must provide a medium through which knowledge is gained. Reference group behaviour must recognize the importance of the norms and values obtained in the group that one must follow. Visibility of norms and role performance is required for the actual behaviour of group members. But it is difficult to have complete knowledge of these norms and actual role performances. It is, argues Merton, mainly based on the structure of the group. At the same time, Merton believes that norms and role performance can be visible if the authority structure is to operate effectively.

   In addition, Merton accepts a limit to the degree of visibility and observability. Here, the notion of 'privacy' is essential to explain this fact. For instance, an authority from a high level would automatically maintain secrecy at work for various reasons. In short, 'reference group theory', argues Merton, 'must systematically incorporate the variable of observability of norms, values and role-performance obtaining in the group as a frame of reference' (Merton, 1957: 411).

2. *Non-conformity as a type of Reference Group Behaviour:* Merton has emphasized: 'that conformist and non-conformist behaviour can be adequately *described*. . ., only if this behaviour is related to the membership groups and non-membership groups taken as frames of normative and evaluative reference' (ibid.).

   Non-conformity, he explains, to the norms of an in-group is equivalent to conformity to the norms of an out-group. In the theory of anomie, he described various ways to understand the person's deviant behaviour in different social structures. As Merton rightly puts it,

   > In the language of reference group theory, therefore, attitudes of conformity to the official mores can be described as a positive orientation to the norms of a non-membership group that is taken as a frame of reference. Such conformity to norms of an out-group is thus equivalent to what is ordinarily called non-conformity, that is, non-conformity to the norms of the in-group (ibid.: 264).

3. *The Structural Context of Reference Group Behaviour: Role-Sets, Status-Sets and Status-Sequences:* In addition to observability and diverse types of non-conformity and deviance in the process of reference group behaviour, it is the need to examine the social structure of roles and statuses and the dynamics of role-sets, status-sets and status-sequences. Ralph Linton has recognized that social status and social roles are fundamental to the description and analysis of a social structure (Linton cites in Merton, 1957: 422).

   > By status, Linton meant a position in a social system occupied by the designated individual, by role, the behavioural enacting of the patterned expectations attributed to that position. In these terms, status and role are concepts that connect the culturally defined expectations with the patterned behaviour and relationships that comprise social structure (Merton, 1957: 422).

Merton defines role-set as a 'particular social status involving not a single associated role but an array of related roles' (Merton, 1957: 423). For instance, a medical student does not associate only with a single status as a student but also a variety of other roles relating to different statuses, such as other students, nurses, physicians, social workers, medical technicians, etc. Here, the concept of role sets is important in reference group theory. However, it can be challenging to satisfy everyone in the role-set. Merton speaks of a 'structural source of instability in the role-set' in this context. Merton outlines, 'the basic source of disturbance in the role-set is the structural circumstance that anyone occupying a particular status has role-partners who are differently located in the social structure' (ibid.: 424).

Merton identified four important mitigating factors at this juncture (Wallace and Wolf, 1980: 58), which reduce the impact of these conflicts or disturbances involved in the role-sets. First, a differential degree of involvement mitigates the effects of diverse role expectations. For instance, in a role set among college students, some are more and some are less involved in their relationship with the student. The second mitigating factor Merton discusses is that those in the role set may compete for power. Still, their involvement in the conflict may 'give the role incumbent more autonomy in some circumstances. Merton's third mechanism to alleviate role conflict is the insulation of role activities from observance by role-set members. The fourth mitigating factor, according to Merton, is the degree to which conflicting demands by members of a role set can be observed. Suppose it is evident that it demands conflict. It is the duty of the members of the role-set and not of the role incumbent to resolve the contradictions. In addition, Merton suggests that mutual social support and withdrawal of control mechanisms would help resolve conflicts of expectations among members of the role-set. This discussion of the role-set illustrates Merton's emphasis on analysing dysfunctional elements and functional alternatives.

In addition to role-sets, the concept of *status-sets* and *status-sequences* also constitute the problem in reference group theory. It is the issue of articulation of the same as that of role-sets. In status-sets, the same individuals may find themselves in different statuses, such as teacher, husband, mother, father, brother, sister, political leader, social worker, author, etc. Every status has its distinctive role set. 'Status-sets provide one basic form of interdependence between the institutions and subsystems of society. This stems from the familiar fact that the same persons are engaged in different social systems' (Merton, 1957: 435).

Merton points out that significant difficulty occurs in organizing their role activities in status-sets. For instance, an administrator may not do justice to his other statuses, such as the status of a husband or the status of a father, because of his commitment to a more significant public cause.

However, Merton suggests how one can avoid the tension in the status-set. First, 'people are not perceived by others as occupying only one status'—second, empathy helps you to understand many others sympathetically. Finally, empathy reduces the pressures exerted upon people caught up in conflicts of status obligation (ibid.: 436). Third, the components of the status-set have reduced the possibility of conflict from both psychological and social viewpoints. As Merton puts it, 'values internalized by people in prior dominant statuses are such as to make it less likely that they will be motivated to enter statuses with values incompati-ble with their own' (ibid.: 437).

According to Merton, *status-sequence* is the observation of sequences of role-sets and status-sets. In this sense, role-sets, status-sets and status-sequences are interlinked and help generate other problems for the functional analysis of social structure.

VI. SCIENCE AND SOCIETY

The relationship between science and society is one of Merton's most influential contributions.. This theme is explored in his essay 'Science and Democratic Social Structure', which is part of his work on *Social Theory and Social Structure.* It is part of his doctoral thesis. On the subject of the sociology of science, he writes, 'the subject matter of the sociology of science is the dynamic inter-dependence of between science, as an ongoing social activity giving rise to cultural and civilizational products and the environing social structure' (Merton, 1957: 585).

The main thrust of Merton's analysis of the sociology of science is to establish the relationship between science and society as the central object of inquiry.

According to Merton, the term 'science', is deceptively inclusive, encompassing a variety of distinct and interrelated elements. As Merton puts it,

> It is commonly used to denote (1) a set of characteristic methods through which knowledge is certified; (2) a stock of accumulated knowledge stemming from the application of these methods; (3) a set of cultural values and mores governing the activities termed scientific; or (4) any combination of the foregoing (ibid.: 605).

His main emphasis here is to outline the cultural structure of science, focusing initially on the institutional aspects of science. Merton argues that the ethos of science has been shaped by complex values and norms that binds the scientist. 'The norms are expressed in the form of prescriptions, proscriptions, preferences and permission. They are legitimatized in terms of institutional values' (ibid.).

The ethos of modern science involves the comparative study of the institutional structure of science. He recognizes that the involvement of various approaches is essential in achieving the institutional goals of science. In this context, Merton outlines,

> The institutional goal of science is the extension of certified knowledge. The technical methods provide the relevant definition of knowledge: empirically confirmed and logically consistent predictions. The institutional imperatives (mores) derive from the goal and the methods. The entire structure of technical and moral norms implements the final objective. The technical norms of empirical evidence, adequate, valid and reliable, are a prerequisite for sustained accurate prediction; the technical norm of logical consistency is a prerequisite for systematic and valid prediction (ibid.: 606).

Therefore, it seems that Merton emphasizes moral and technical prescriptions for the institutional ethos of science.

Merton describes four sets of institutional imperatives, i.e., universalism, communism, disinterestedness organized scepticism and the ethos of science. *Universalism* refers to that truth which 'are to be subjected to *pre-established, impersonal criteria*: consonant with observation and with previously confirmed knowledge' (Merton, 1957: 607).

The acceptance or rejection of truth within science does not depend on personal or social attributes. Universalism is mainly based on objectivity and scientifically verified formulations of any event or phenomenon. However, the institution of science is not always integrated with a more significant part of the social structure. As a result, the larger culture opposes universalism and science's ethos is severely strained. For instance, ethnocentrism is incompatible with universalism (ibid.). Here, Merton acknowledges the importance of democracy, in which universalism is a dominant guiding principle.

'Communism', according to Merton, is a second integral element of the scientific ethos. It is, in general terms, used in the sense of shared ownership of goods. In communism, 'they constitute a common heritage in which the equity of the individual producer is severely limited' (ibid.: 610).

Scientists' communal character of science is recognized for their dependence upon a cultural heritage. However, Merton acknowledges that 'the communism of the scientific ethos is incompatible with the definition of technology as "private property" in a capitalist economy' (ibid.: 612).

'Disinterestedness' is a third element of the ethos of science. In general, science includes disinterestedness as a basic institutional element. As Merton puts it, 'The demand for disinterestedness has a firm basis in the public and testable character of science, and this circumstance, it may be supposed, has contributed to the integrity of men of science' (ibid.: 613).

'Organized scepticism' is the fourth and last element of the scientific ethos. It is related to both a methodological and institutional mandate. Every aspect of nature and society related to science may conflict with other attitudes of institutions, such as rituals, the sacred and the profane, etc. In this sense, Merton says, 'conflict becomes accentuated whenever science extends its research to new areas toward which there are institutionalized attitudes or other institutions extend their area of control' (Merton, 1957: 615).

Merton's analysis of the sociology of science in terms of relations between science and society is incomplete. However, it provides a new direction for sociologists to think about it. Joseph Ben-David, a sociologist of science, accepted his work as one of the essential books in the sociology of science.

VIII. CONCLUSION

Robert K. Merton is considered the most outstanding American sociologist who has contributed significantly to sociological concepts, theories and methods of sociology. From the 1940s to the 1960s, Merton became mainstream in American Sociology. His contributions to sociology include sociology, functional approach, social system and structure, sociological theory and social change and its related themes. Merton considered sociology to be a scientific discipline. In this sense, he tries to bridge the hiatus between sociological theory and empirical research. Merton illustrates his application of sociological theory and empirical research to the theory of *reference group, anomie* and *nature of science* or *ethos of science.* In addition, Merton's most important theoretical orientations are theories of the middle range, paradigm, the self-fulfilling prophecy, anticipatory socialization, the role-set, manifest and latent function, etc.

Merton has followed a functional approach to analyse the social structure of society. The important fact related to Merton's available analysis is that his functionalism is in time and space and deals with empirical reality. In functional analysis, he points out the problems of structural functionalism and conceptual confusion. He formulates three postulates and provides a broader conceptual framework, such as function, dysfunction, nonfunction, latent and manifest function, to understand and analyse functionalism precisely.

Merton has also dealt with the concepts of *role, status, social structure, social system, group,* etc. These are the basic units for understanding the nature of society. However, he gives more emphasis on social structure. Merton considers social and psychological factors when defining a social structure, status, and role. Merton's psychological emphasis can be seen in the analysis of membership groups and his concept of *anticipatory socialization.* In the theoretical analysis, Merton takes a middle path between macro and micro theories in middle-range theory. In middle-range theories, conceptual abstractions emerge from the need to understand certain concrete empirical situations. In this context, Merton is very cautious about the formulation of the problem and the empirical verification of hypotheses. He also pays special attention to the construction of theory. Therefore, he provides tools of logical classification called *paradigms* for constructing theory.

However, Merton has been criticized for his theoretical, methodological and conceptual understanding. First, many later sociologists accuse him of neglecting the unique historical and symbolic features of social reality that require entirely different study methods than what is available through empirical methods of science. The second point of criticism is that he has emphasized functionalism based on agreement or consensus and social order principles. However, Merton has discussed the various ways of arising out of *strain* and conflict among the members of society. Despite his criticism, Merton has maintained the quality of his writings. He is a serious and thoughtful scholar and a superb sociologist and he has illuminated every subject to which he has directed his attention.

KEY TERMS

Conformity: Merton has discussed the term in his theory of deviance. The term 'usually denotes conformity to the norms and expectations current in the individual's membership group . . . conformity to norms of an out-group is thus equivalent to what is ordinarily called non-conformity, that is, non-conformity to the norms of the in-group' (R.K. Merton). In short, it is people's behaviour according to a social group's expectations.

Deviance: Non-conformity to social norms. Deviance is very natural in the life of every human being.

Dysfunction: The term was introduced by R.K. Merton in the analysis of the functional approach. It refers to any consequence of the existence or operation of an aspect of a social (or personality) system that is judged to be a disturbance or a hindrance to the system's integration, adjustment or stability.

Empathy: The ability to project oneself imaginatively into another's position, that is, to understand or take another person's role without losing objectivity.

Empirical: Based on experience, observation or experimentation.

Frame of Reference: It is a point of view, standard or system of concepts held by an individual (or group) that tends to organize experiences, perceptions and interpretations.

Function, Latent: A functional relation that is neither intended nor recognized. Robert K. Merton introduced the term. It refers to 'unintended and unrecognized consequences. . . . For a specified unit (person, subgroup, social or cultural system) which contribute to its adjustment or adaptation'. Merton used the Hopi rain dance as an example. The manifest function of the rain dance is to bring rain. However, such ceremonies also 'fulfil the latent function of reinforcing the group identity by providing a periodic occasion on which the scattered members of a group assemble to engage in a common activity' (R.K. Merton).

Function, Manifest: A functional relation having a recognized value. R.K. Merton introduced the term in contradiction to latent function. It refers to 'those objective consequences for a specified unit (person, subgroup, social or cultural system) which contribute to its adjustment or adaptation and were so intended' (R.K. Merton).

In-group: Any group whose membership has a strong sense of identification, loyalty and exclusiveness toward non-members.

Innovation: It is one of the types of Merton's theory of deviance or anomic. It refers to developing new elements or patterns in a culture without taking care of institutional means.

Non-conformity: Behaviour perceived as divergent from social expectations in a particular situation. Non-conformity is a relative concept, and an act that violates the norms in one situation or group may conform with the norms of other groups.

Paradigm: The term has been used by R.K. Merton to refer to deviance for presenting as a succinct codification of an area of sociological analysis. Thus, a paradigm is a compact outline of the central concepts, assumptions, procedures, propositions and problems of a substantive area or a theoretical approach in sociological analysis.

Rebellion: It is also one of five adaptation modes, as Merton discussed. It involves rejecting the culturally prescribed goals and the institutionalized means of achieving them, substituting new goals and means.

Reference Group: The concept of reference group was introduced by Herbert H. Hyman in his book *Archives of Psychology* and discussed by R.K. Merton. A reference group is a group or social category that an individual uses to help define his beliefs, attitudes and values and guide his behaviour.

Reference group, Negative: A group whose norms and activities an individual uses to guide what he shall reject and oppose. R.K. Merton also discusses it in his theory of reference groups.

Reference group, Positive: The term positive reference group is synonymous with a reference group.

Relative Deprivation: The term was initially used by Samuel A. Stouffer in *The American Soldier.* It is a relative term measured not by objective standards but by comparison the relatively superior advantages of others.

Retreatism: The term was used by R.K. Merton in his typology of individual modes of adaptation to patterns of cultural goals and institutional norms to refer to one of five modes of adaptation. It is a form of deviant behaviour in which the individual rejects the culturally defined goals of success of the standardized means of attaining them.

Ritualism: It is a type of individual adaptation in which the individual rejects culturally defined goals because he feels he cannot succeed in attaining them but continues to cling to the institutionalized routines and norms that are supposed to lead to these goals. Thus, ritualism is one of five modes of adaptation to patterns of cultural goals and institutional norms.

Role Model: Merton used it in the analysis of reference group theory. The role model differs from the *reference individual.* The *internalization* of the role model's standards of behaviour and attitudes is limited to one or a very few roles. In contrast, *identification* with a reference individual is more comprehensive, including a wide range of roles.

Role-set: It is defined by R.K. Merton as a set of roles that centres around a particular *social status.* Any given social status involves an individual actor (person) in several social relationships that are always or usually necessary for persons in that specific status.

Self-fulfilling Prophecy: The concept was developed by R.K. Merton based on W.I. Thomas' statement: 'If men define situations as accurate, they are real in their consequences.' This is also known as the Thomas theorem. A self-fulfilling prophecy is a false definition of a situation or belief regarding a social situation. Because one believes and acts upon it, it manifests as truth, further strengthening that belief.

Social Category: A plurality of persons not organized into a system of social interaction but with similar social characteristics or statuses. However, most social categories do not develop into a group.

Socialization, Anticipatory: The term was introduced by R.K. Merton and Alice S. Kitt. Merton explains *anticipatory socialization* in the context of non-membership reference groups. It involves preparing oneself for the group to which an individual aspires and adopts the values and lifestyles but does not belong.

Status Sequence: A 'succession of statuses occurring with sufficient frequency as to be socially patterned . . . as in the case, for example, of the statuses successively occupied by a medical student, intern, resident and independent medical practitioner. In much the same sense, of course, we can observe *sequences of role-sets* and *status-sets*' (R.K. Merton).

Status-set: As defined by R.K. Merton, the complex of different and distinct statuses occupied by a single individual. Therefore, a person's status set changes when any one of his various statuses changes and thus represents a person's status only at one particular moment.

REFERENCES

Abraham, M. Francis, *Modern Sociological Theory: An Introduction*, Oxford: Oxford University Press, 2000.

Bierstedt, Robert, *American Sociological Theory: A Critical History*, New York: Academic Press, 1981.

Handel, Warren H., *Contemporary Sociological Theory*, Englewood Cliffs: Prentice-Hall, Inc., 1993.

Haralambos, M., *Sociology: Themes and Perspectives*, Oxford: Oxford University Press, 1999.

Merton, Robert K., 'Introduction to Social Theory and Social Structure', in Jeffrey Alexander, Raymond Boudon and Mohamed Cherkaoui (eds.), *The Classical Tradition in Sociology, The American Tradition*, vol. II, London: Sage Publications, 1997, pp. 333-48.

——, *Social Theory and Social Structure*, New York: Free Press of Glencoe, 1957.

Merton, Robert K. and Alice S. Kitt, 'Contributions to the Theory of Reference Group Behaviour', in Jeffrey Alexandar, Raymond Boudon and Mohamed Cherkaoui (eds.).

Miles, Mary Wilson, 'The Writings of Robert K. Merton: A Bibliography', in Coser (ed.), *The Idea of Social Structure, Papers in Honour of Robert K. Merton*, New York: Harcourt Brace Jovanovich, 1975, pp. 497-516.

Parsons, Talcott, 'On Building Social System Theory: A Personal History', *Daedalus*, 1970, pp. 826-81.

Turner, Jonathan H., *The Structure of Sociological Theory*, Homewood: The Dorsey Press, 1978.

Wallace, Ruth A. and Alison Wolf, *Contemporary Sociological Theory: Continuing the Classical Tradition*, Englewood Cliffs: Prentice-Hall, Inc., 1980.

CHAPTER 3

Phenomenology

INTRODUCTION AND ORIGIN

Hegel first discussed phenomenology in his work *Phenomenology of Mind* in 1807. The word, derived from the conjunction of the noun form of *phainomai* appears and *logos* or reason. Phenomenological sociology, therefore, deals with the reason for appearance. *The Encyclopedia of Sociology* defines phenomenology as:

a method in philosophy that begins with the individual and his own conscious experience and tries to avoid prior assumptions, prejudices and philosophical dogmas. Phenomenology thus examines phenomena as they are apprehended in their 'immediacy' by the social actor (Wallace and Wolf, 1980: 233).

The primary focus of phenomenological sociology is the act of understanding. In this context, in phenomenology, 'the capacity of the human mind to understand meaning is more basic than either formal logic or the modes in which knowledge is articulated or structured' (Mitchel, 1999: 141).

The phenomenological approach, therefore, emphasizes not taking the notions for granted. It means one must question his social situation by suspending or 'bracketing' his learned cultural concepts.

The basic proposition states that everyday reality is a socially constructed system of ideas accumulated over time and is taken for granted by group members. This perspective takes a critical stance about the social order and, in contrast to functionalism, challenges our culturally learned ideas (Wallace and Wolf, 1980: 233).

Hence, phenomenological perspectives in sociology offer a radical alternative to the functional approach in a theoretical sense and positivists in a methodological sense. This perspective starts with the difference between natural science and social science subject matter and methodology. In this sense, discussing its historical roots of emergence is essential. Some scholars, such as Dilthey, Windelband and Rickert, had made significant contributions to the emergence of phenomenology. However, the primary source of the phenomenological tradition in modern times is the work and ideas of Max Weber, Edmund Husserl and Alfred Schutz.

The phenomenological approach has its roots in the debate on the applicability of the scientific method, as described in the natural sciences, to the study of society. This debate has been mainly discussed by Wilhelm Dilthey, Windelband, Rickert and Weber, which profoundly influenced Alfred Schutz's understanding of phenomenology. Dilthey points out a fundamental difference between studying nature (*Naturwissenschaften*) and studying society (*Geistewissenschaften*) because of the different subject matters associated with the various disciplines.

> With natural science, we uncover the kingdom of nature: objective, inanimate, existing entirely apart from humanity. On the other hand, studying society involves investigating the kingdom of the human mind, where all cultural phenomena are mental products of a human consciousness that is subjective and immersed in emotion and intellect (Gorman, 1997: 174).

The natural sciences deal with matter but not human consciousness, while the social sciences are related to human consciousness. Windelband and Rickert, on the other hand, discussed two methods of investigation. First, it explains phenomena by laying down broad covering laws of universal applicability (ibid.: 175). This method of inquiry, which Windelband terms 'nomothetic' and Rickert 'generalizing', uncovers the general laws of natural science. The second method of investigation is the opposite method of explaining unique phenomena according to characteristics that make the phenomena unique in the first place (ibid.: 175). This method, which Windelband calls 'ideographic' and Rickert 'individualizing', focuses on describing unique events in their concreteness and individuality. 'Thus, a distinction is made between the natural sciences that seek to establish general laws and the cultural sciences that isolate individual phenomena to trace their unique development' (Aron, 1967: 68).

In this connection, Max Weber accepts the logical separation of natural and cultural science of Windelband and Rickert but rejects their different contention methods to classify these sciences (Weber, 1949). Weber feels that every science can use both (i.e. nomothetic or generalizing and ideographic or individualizing) methods depending on the discipline's research goals (Gorman, 1997: 176). In this sense, Weber accepts a significant difference between the natural and social sciences subject matters. For example, in sociology, we can use the generalizing method in empirical research and biology or astronomy, it occasionally studies unique aspects of phenomena. But this fact seems to be a complex issue. However, Weber tries to illustrate his approach to this complex issue with the help of the concept of 'value-relevance' (*Wertbeziehung*).

> Whereas in the natural sciences, we investigate abstract concepts which are quantitatively measured, in the study of human affairs what we define as significant (object deemed worthy of study) is constituted by values we implicitly or explicitly accept (Gorman, 1997: 177).

Thus, natural sciences are concerned with objectivity, while social sciences are necessarily related to value-oriented and subjectivity. Therefore, Weber accepts the utility of the scientific method but raises the question of how it is used. As Weber puts it,

> by utilizing the natural scientific method to study society, we neglect precisely those issues important from a social point of view, concentrating instead on the regular, mechanistic-type behaviour we regularly perform in our daily lives but rarely think or care about (Weber cites in Gorman, 1997: 178).

Therefore, using natural scientific methods to study human behaviour will be irrelevant and unimportant.

Weber's concept of *Verstehen* or 'interpretative understanding', is central to phenomenological sociology. He proposes this concept to explain how an event is unique rather than general without sacrificing the explanation of scientific validity. The goal of *verstehen* is to recreate the meaning observed actors experience now of action. At this point, phenomenological sociology seems quite close to Weber's concept of *verstehen.*

I. EDMUND HUSSERL (1859-1938)

Husserl laid the foundation of modern phenomenology. Due to this, he is often regarded as the father of phenomenology. His phenomenological approach appears in his most notable philosophical treatise, *Ideas: Introduction to Pure Phenomenology* (1913). The phenomenological approach of Husserl is based upon a particular philosophical foundation known as *transcendental phenomenology.* Transcendental phenomenology is dominated by Husserl's search for the essential foundations of knowledge in experience: an endeavour to formulate a basis for expertise 'free from presuppositions' (Mitchel, 1999: 141). Husserl defined phenomenology as interest in those things that one's sense can directly apprehend (Wallace and Wolf, 1980: 234). Husserl's phenomenology is considered a philosophical movement. His philosophy aims to accurately describe all world aspects as they appear in the subject's consciousness. Consciousness, therefore, is central to his phenomenological understanding. But he concludes, 'consciousness itself has a being of its own which in its absolute uniqueness of nature remains unaffected by the phenomenological disconnection' (Husserl cites in Gorman, 1997: 188).

In this sense, consciousness involves philosophical inquiry that attempts to understand how this process operates and how it influences human affairs. Humans, therefore, know the world only through experience.

> All notions of an external world, 'out there', are mediated through the senses and can only be known through mental consciousness. Experiences always mediate other people, values, norms and physical objects as they register people's conscious awareness. One does not directly contact reality; contact is always indirect and mediated through the human mind processes (Turner, J., 1978: 395).

Therefore, consciousness becomes the central concern of phenomenology in creating the experience of an external reality.

In reviewing Husserl's phenomenology, several features of his work come out. These are:

(*i*) *The Concept of Psychologism:* Husserl considered himself an advocate of a philosophical movement known as *psychologism.* He believed here, psychology is the basis of all human interpretations of valid knowledge. At this point, Husserl was influenced by Franz Brentano. Brentano was considered the primary motivator of Husserl's philosophical thinking. Due to Brentano's influential lectures, he abandoned mathematics for a career in philosophy.

(*ii*) *The Idea of Intentionality:* The idea of intentionality is created by Brentano to distinguish between mental or psychological activities (such as thinking, desiring, hating, etc.) and physical phenomena. Psychology is concerned with describing the nature of consciousness and tries to concentrate on the subject. Husserl thinks about the structure of consciousness and the relationship between consciousness and objectivity in the concept of intentionality. Husserl discusses 'the dual goals of closely analysing the intentional structure of consciousness and describing objects as they present themselves to consciousness' in the phenomenological study (Gorman, 1997: 186). He believes our experiences are generally more complex, so we cannot get objective knowledge. Instead, Husserl suggests that these complex experiences must be broken down into their intentional component act and arrive at their meaning as constituted in our actual life experience. Husserl calls this investigative method 'intentional analysis'.

(*iii*) *The Notion of 'Epoche':* Husserl systematical suspends belief in the world, worldly objects and statements concerning knowledge of the world (ibid.: 188). This belief led him to the notion of *epoche or* bracketing of the world. Observers also suspend belief in their mundane existences. The *epoche* thus eliminates any personal position or attitude relating to factual existence. In this sense, *epoche* prevents impure empirical facts from intruding.

The entire process of suspending belief in the world and one's self expresses what Husserl means by *phenomenological reduction.* As it is actualized, the natural, commonsense world we live and act in is 'reduced' or purified, into one devoid of subjective or empirical assumptions (ibid.).

(*iv*) *Transcendental Ego:* In the earlier writings, Husserl's emphasis on pure description precluded the possibility of an ego existing behind acts of consciousness. Contrary to that, he discovers the pure or transcendental ego, which pervades all acts and objects of consciousness, giving sense and validity to the world and constituting the world's meaning (Husserl, E., 1931: 51-97 and 147-84). The transcendental ego connects the subjectivity of perception to the objectivity of a universally accepted epistemology.

(*v*) *The Concept of 'Lebenswelt': Lebenswelt* or lifeworld constitutes a theme of Husserl's phenomenological philosophy. Husserl's primary intention here is to distinguish between the *mundane* and Lebenswelt worlds. The *Lebenswelt* refers to the locus of reflective social action. 'The *Lebenswelt* is an intersubjective world because we implicitly assume the existence and similar experiences of interacting individuals' (Gorman, 1997: 192).

Therefore, the lifeworld is concerned with pre-reflective experience in everyday life. This 'lifeworld' is also called the 'world of the natural attitude'. Turner summarizes two main features of Husserl's conception of the 'lifeworld' as follows:

1. The 'lifeworld' is taken for granted. It is rarely the topic of reflective thought, yet it structures and shapes how people act and think.
2. Humans operate on the assumption that they experience the same world. Since each person experiences only their consciousness, the individual has little capacity to determine if this presumption is correct directly. Yet, people act as if they experienced an ordinary world (Turner, J., 1978: 396).

The notion of 'lifeworld' then becomes the foundation of modern phenomenology that emphasizes two things: taken-for-granted knowledge and collective experience. Human activity, therefore, conducted in a lifeworld is considered taken for granted and presumed to be experienced collectively.

Methods of Scientific Investigation: Husserl (Gorman, 1997: 193-4) describes two possible methods of scientific inquiry in the pre-reflective lifeworld. The first is the ontological analysis of *Lebenswelt,* which focuses on pre-reflective attitudes and the essential nature of consciousness. According to Husserl, the second methods involve a process of transcendental phenomenological analysis that concentrates on bracketing the Lebenswelt itself and stressing a broader constitution of the essence by the transcendental ego. In his philosophical understanding of transcendental phenomenology, observers can synthesize objective and subjective levels of reality.

Husserl's philosophical doctrine of transcendental phenomenology has failed to develop an abstract theory of consciousness. However, his ideas provided a new line of thought, becoming the basis of modern phenomenology and ethnomethodology. We can summarize his fundamental ideas in the words of Turner (Turner, J., 1978: 397) as follows:

1. The emphasis on the abstract process of consciousness stimulated thinkers to inquire into how the basic mental processes of individuals shape the nature of the social world. Thus, rather than viewing the world as imposed upon consciousness, concern shifted to how it is created out of the subjective processes of the human mind.
2. The concern with creating a 'lifeworld' led scholars to question how humans create a sense of reality and how this sense of reality, as opposed to some real external world, can be the main ingredient in revolving around the problem of order.
3. The critique of social science has served others in phenomenology who suggest that an objective science of humans may not be possible or at the very least, will not be the same as the science of the physical world.
4. The failure of Husserl's radical solution appears to have convinced phenomenologists that understanding human consciousness and social reality can only occur by examining individuals in actual interaction (not in bracketed, radical abstraction).

Husserl's phenomenology, then, was a major philosophical programme aimed at disclosing the absolute ground of human knowledge. Dickens remarks:

Husserl's fully developed philosophy may be characterized as a philosophical hermeneutic aimed at disclosing the absolute grounds of human knowledge through a bringing to light of the unexpressed presuppositions which characterize that knowledge (Dickens, 1979: 345).

II. ALFRED SCHUTZ (1899-1959)

Alfred Schutz (1899-1959) was a social philosopher and phenomenologist. His phenomenological ideas in social sciences are well accepted and recognized by other social scientists and sociologists. However, Schutz's phenomenological work originates in the work of German scholars (Rickert, Windelband, Dilthey and Weber), Husserl's transcendental phenomenology and American interactionism. Schutz's work, therefore, is considered eclectic.

Schutz's ideas, like those of Rickert, Windelband and Weber before him, are efforts at building bridges between those who insist upon the unique, even spiritual, quality of human behaviour and those believing it is only by subsuming behaviour under inclusive, empirically confirmed laws that valid social knowledge is possible (Gorman, 1997: 195). Schutz's main aim here is to preserve the integrity of unique subjects without sacrificing the exactness and clarity of empirical scientific explanation. Schutz begins his theoretical analysis by questioning the *Verstehen* approach of Weber. *Verstehen's* approach is incomplete for the following reasons: (a) It does not consider common sense knowledge; (b) It is unclear what sense he is talking of meanings; and (c) How the other actor perceives another person with his subjective meaning. However, Schutz accepts Weber's insistence on the importance of the empirical scientific method. He also agrees with the three main concepts of Weber's methodology: value-relevance, *Verstehen* and the ideal type. Schutz corrected this when he used these concepts in his analysis.

Husserl's phenomenology profoundly influenced Schutz. He accepts Husserl's notion of *Lebenswelt,* i.e., lifeworld, that prereflective world of everyday existence in which meanings and values are unquestioningly accepted (Gorman, 1997: 196). In other words, humans hold a 'natural attitude' and 'lifeworld' that is taken for granted and shapes who they are and what they will do.

However, Schutz rejects Husserl's understanding of transcendental ego and its absolute correlative knowledge that emphasizes the merging of subjectivity and objectivity and simultaneously accepts Husserl's belief in the supremacy of the individual, subjective consciousness in formulating the meaning each person experiences (Gorman, 1997: 194-5). Schutz's main emphasis here is to eliminate Husserl's understanding of objectivity.

Schutz's phenomenology also came under the influence of early symbolic interactionists, particularly G.H. Mead and W.I. Thomas' due to his immigration to the United States.

> The early symbolic interactionist's concern with constructing shared meanings was similar to Schutz's desire to understand intersubjectivity. Schutz thus found an immediate affinity with W.I. Thomas' concept of 'definition of the situation' since this concept emphasizes that actors construct orientation to and dispositions to act in situations (Turner, J., 1978: 400).

Thomas' definitions of situations appear in Schutz's conceptualization of the process of intersubjectivity. In addition, Schutz was also influenced by George Herbert Mead's conceptual analysis of role-taking, generalized others and the process of interaction. Schutz was impressed with Mead's view that the mind is a social process in the interaction. Another influence on Schutz is Mead's concept of role-taking, by which actors assume the attitude of others through the interpretation of gestures. Role-taking helps construct the Schutzian concept of 'typification' whereby actors come to know each other's role and typify each other in interaction. Additionally, Mead's concept of the 'generalized other' may have influenced Schutz because actors share a 'community of attitudes' or common subjective states.

Having reviewed some critical intellectual influences on Schutz, it is now possible to provide his phenomenological scheme and its implications for sociological theorizing. First, his analysis of Weber, Husserl and interactionism led him to think on many key issues: (1) How do actors create an everyday subjective world? (2) What implications does this creation have for maintaining social order? (3) What is the social reality with which sociologists concern themselves?

SCHUTZ'S PHENOMENOLOGICAL ORIENTATION

Schutz's phenomenological work appears in his major work, *The Phenomenology of the Social World,* published in 1932. His phenomenological work also deals in his three papers: Volume One, *The Problem of Social Reality* (1962); Volume Two, *Studies in Social Theory* (1964); and Volume Three, *Studies in Phenomenological Philosophy* (1966). As pointed out by Schutz, the primary aim of propounding this work is

> Orthodox Sociology has failed to recognize the significance of the everyday world of commonsense beliefs and practices as the basis of social reality. In studying how social actors 'typify' actions and employ 'stock of knowledge' to create a meaningful social world, we can open a new dimension to sociology (Mitchel, 1999: 142).

His contribution to phenomenology focuses on the structure and functioning of consciousness and the social world as mental constructs. In other words, Schutz asserts that all humans carry rules, social recipes, conceptions of appropriate conduct and other information that allows them to act in their social world (Turner, 1978: 401). He argued that sociologists should examine commonsense beliefs and actions. He has applied his ideas to literary criticism, musical appreciation, politics and the sociology of knowledge. Schutz asserted the importance of studying how interaction creates and maintains a 'paramount reality'. He was also concerned with how actors achieve interchange of perspectives and construct a taken-for-granted world that gives order to social life. We can outline his phenomenological contribution to sociology in the following points in a conceptual form:

(*i*) *Meaning and Intersubjectivity:* Schutz believed that the 'experience and assumption of shared meanings built the foundation which made social life possible'. For this, he discusses two levels of meaning. The first level of significance, which Schutz defines as meaning in its 'primordial' sense, is constituted by the individual's consciousness. But on the other, it means on a second level, in which social actors directly experience each other. Thus, meaning on the second level is constituted by interaction between individuals in the social world. In this context, phenomenological sociology must be based on 'the way meaning is constituted in the individual experience of the solitary Ego. In so doing, we shall track meaning to its very point of origin in the inner time consciousness in the duration of the ego as it lives through its experience' (Schutz, 1967: 13).

Schutz was focused on how people grasp the consciousness of others while they live within their stream of consciousness. In other words, when two individuals share a single experience, the meaning constituted in that activity is called intersubjective in a literal sense. His examination of the phenomena of intersubjective understanding is concerned primarily with explaining how the interaction between individuals in the social world takes place on many levels of anonymity. Schutz uses the differences in the levels of anonymity in social experiences to classify various encounters in the social world (ibid.: 163-86)). He asserts that the different levels of anonymity on which the individual experiences others in the social world create the structure or 'regions' of that world. He employs a full range of conceptual tools which facilitate the analysis of these structures: the face-to-face relationship, we and they relationship and the worlds of predecessors and contemporaries (For details about different types of relationships, see Schutz's analysis of the social world, next to it).

(*ii*) *Typification and Uniqueness:* Two significant elements in social relations, typification and uniqueness, become a focus of Schutz's analysis. 'Schutz views individuals as constructing a world by using the typifications (or ideal types) passed on to them by their social group' (Wallace and Wolf, 1980: 235).

Schutz is much more explicit on this fundamental point than Weber. He clearly states that social scientists must begin with a commonsense understanding of the social actors. He emphasizes that the social scientist's ideal types should be synthesized using these understandings as a base. His principal point is that the ideal type of social scientist is 'second-order constructs' because they are built on the social actor's concept;

thus, they are 'preselected and reinterpreted' by the social actor's understanding (Schutz, 1962: 5). In typification, actors use their stock of knowledge to categorize each other and to adjust their responses to this typification. Hence, actors can effectively deal with their world. In face-to-face relations, typification is necessarily modified by the unique situation. Thus, the rule of thumb is that the more personal the relationship, the more typified (Abraham, 2000: 251).

(*iii*) *Reciprocity of Perspectives:* For Schutz, the individual's meaning of a situation in everyday life is of prime importance; he puts the spotlight on the individual's definition of the situation (Wallace and Wolf, 1980: 235). He believes that the meaning an individual imparts to the interaction situation may be shared by the person with whom they are interacting; Schutz calls this 'reciprocity of perspectives'. Wallace and Wolf give an example of an orchestra to explain the idea of 'reciprocity of perspectives'. Because the musicians in an orchestra share the meanings of the situation with the conductor, they could exchange positions with the conductor and experience the situation the way the conductor did. 'Shared meanings', Wallace and Wolf (1980: 235-6) explain, 'maybe both assumed and experienced in the interaction situation. In these situations, people are acting based on taken-for-granted assumptions about reality'.

(*iv*) *Multiple-Reality:* Schutz argued that there are many realities, each with its own 'attitude' or 'style of existence'. He advances the thesis of William James's theory of multiple reality that all human experiences occur in one of many 'finite provinces of reality', each defined by a particular cognitive style that gives experiences in that province their distinct 'accent of reality'. Schutz specifies several criteria by which the cognitive style of one province of reality is distinguished from another: each has its own 'tension of consciousness', the experience of self, a form of sociality and perspective of time (Schutz, 1962: 230). Examples of these provinces of reality, which Schutz discusses, are the commonsense world of social action, the world of dreams, the world of religious experience and the world of scientific theorizing. Several discussions of multiple realities involved understanding how Schutz conceptualizes social scientific theorizing and the relationship between that activity and the world of social action. First, he argues that one of these finite provinces of reality, the commonsense world of social action, can be labelled as 'paramount reality'. Second, Schutz contends that each of these provinces is 'finite', meaning that each is experienced separately and that transition from one to another always involves a 'shock'. Third, although there are multiple realities, they are not equally fundamental. Schutz called the reality of everyday life the most fundamental reality that gears into the real world.

(v) *Lifeworld or* Lebenswelt: Husserl's vision of *Lebeneswelt* is central to Schutz's phenomenological sociology. This is an intersubjective world in which people create social reality and are constrained by their predecessors' preexisting social and cultural structures. Schutz is more interested in dealing with the specific elements of the lifeworld that are part of the taken-for-granted reality of everyday life. These components are—knowledge of skills, helpful knowledge and knowledge of recipes (Ritzer, 1988: 336-7). Each is part of the social stock of knowledge and leads to habitual action. First, *knowledge of skills* is the most basic form of knowledge in that it rarely becomes problematic and thus is accorded a high degree of certainty. The skill of walking is an example of knowledge of skills. Second, *useful knowledge* is a definite solution to a problem that was once problematic. Although this type of knowledge is not trustworthy, it has achieved a high level of certainty. Examples include courses of action, such as driving a car or playing the piano.

Knowledge of recipes, the third form of customary knowledge, is the most variable but still standardized. In certain situations, recipes are called forth as standard ways to cope. Whenever possible, an actor employs a recipe. For instance, in dealing with most customers, a salesperson can use time-tested techniques. However, should the situation become problematic and the customer behaves in unusual ways, the salesperson can employ an alternative recipe or develop an innovative response. Within the lifeworld, Schutz differentiated between intimate face-to-face relationships ('we-relations') and distant and impersonal relationships ('they relations'). While face-to-face relations are of great importance in the life-world, it is far easier for sociologists to study more impersonal relations scientifically. Although Schutz turned away from consciousness and the intersubjective lifeworld, he did offer insights into consciousness, especially in his thoughts on the meaning and people's motives.

In short, phenomenology is considered a branch of social science that explains phenomena with significant meaning to our lives. People like Hegel, Husserl and so on have superseded the phenomenological tradition. Alfred Schutz made this phrase famous in the English world. The phenomenological tradition also had to eradicate the general feelings of facts and get into the inner reality of life. Schutz is concerned with the dialectical relationship between how people construct social reality and the obdurate social and cultural reality they inherit from those who preceded them in the social world.

SCHUTZ'S ANALYSIS OF THE SOCIAL WORLD

Schutz identified four distinct realms of social reality. Every type of social world is based on and distinguished by its degree of immediacy (the degree to which situations are within reach of the actor) and determinability (the degree to which the actor can control them). The four realms of the social world are *umwelt,* the realm of directly experienced social reality; *mitwelt,* the realm of indirectly experienced social reality; *folgewelt,* the realm of successors; and *vorwelt,* the realm of predecessors. The realms of successors and predecessors (*folgewelt* and *vorwelt*) are of peripheral interest to Schutz. Now, we begin with the discussion of *umwelt.*

Umwelt: Umwelt is central to Schutz's work of the social world. It refers to the realm of directly experienced social reality. 'Within the realm of immediate experience, the social construction of reality takes place and the scientist has a good chance of understanding it' (Schutz, 1962: 331).

In this sense, the actor's experience within immediate social reality would involve the actor's consciousness and face-to-face interaction. In *umwelt,* in Schutz's view, actors would have considerable freedom and creativity and therefore, unpredictable actor is outside the realm of scientific sociology (Schutz, 1962: 331). However, Schutz went on to say that we can ignore 'the ultimate roots of the action in the person's consciousness' (Schutz, 1967: 190).

On the other hand, Schutz has confusion about face-to-face interaction in the *umwelt.* All people have minds and, therefore, are unpredictable in face-to-face interaction. Schutz, thus, is inclined to eliminate face-to-face interaction from scientific sociology due to the involvement of mental processes. Here, Schutz says that the *umwelt* cannot be part of the science of sociology and hence, his definition of sociology excludes real actors and their minds and *umwelt.* Instead of looking at the *umwelt,* Schutz focused on *mitwelt* or the realm of contemporaries whom sociologists do not encounter as actual individuals but merely as types.

Mitwelt: The *mitwelt* is more central to Schutz's work. The *mitwelt* refers to the realm of indirectly experienced social reality. Ritzer points out,

> The *mitwelt* is that aspect of the social world in which people ordinarily deal with types of people or larger social structures rather than with actual actors. People do fill these types and these structures, but these people are rarely experienced directly (Ritzer, 1988: 332).

Actors are concerned with more extensive social structures, so their knowledge is not subject to constant revision based on face-to-face interaction. Due to this relatively constant knowledge, actors can study the social world scientifically. 'The *mitwelt* is a stratified world with levels arranged by degree of anonymity. The more anonymous the level, the more people's relationships are amenable to scientific study' (ibid.).

Folgewelt: The future (*folgewelt*) is a purely residual category in Schutz's work. 'It is a totally free and completely indeterminate world that is not dominated by any scientific laws. The social scientist can only anticipate it very generally and cannot be pictured in any detail' (Ritzer, 1988: 331).

Due to its indeterminate quality, it fails to observe outside from reach of the actor.

Vorwelt: The past (*vorwelt*) refers to the realm of predecessors and is partially amenable to scientific analysis. 'The action of those who lived in the past is totally determined; there is no element of freedom because the causes of their actions, the actions themselves and their outcomes have already occurred' (ibid.).

However, despite its determinacy quality, the study of predecessors presents difficulties for subjective sociology because it is difficult to interpret the actions of people who lived in an earlier time with the help of contemporary categories of thought that we use presently. In this sense, the interpretation of contemporaries is likely more accurate because sociologists share interpretive categories with those whose actions they seek to understand.

In a nutshell, Schutz describes every type of social world but is more interested in eliminating two from social scientific considerations. He eliminated the worlds of directly experienced associates (*umwelt*) and successors (*folgewelt*) from the scientific sociological study because actors' freedom is present. Predecessors (*vorwelt*) lack freedom and are, therefore, a proper subject of subjective sociology. Thus, the world of contemporaries (*mitwelt*) is the most amenable to social scientific study. This is true because (1) it is dominated by types and structures rather than free and unpredictable actors, and (2) the scientist lives in that world; they can better understand the structures and the types that exist in it.

III. THE SOCIAL CONSTRUCTION OF REALITY: BERGER AND LUCKMANN

The work of Peter Berger and Thomas Luckmann represents another vital branch of phenomenological sociology. Berger and Luckmann tried to extend the concerns of phenomenological sociology to social structures and institutions. In the *Social Construction of Reality* (1967), Berger and Luckmann take the sociology of knowledge approach and integrate the individual and societal levels. The focus is on the 'processes by which *any* body' knowledge' comes to be socially accepted *as* 'reality' (Berger and Luckmann, 1967: 3). By 'reality construction', authors mean the process whereby people continuously create, through their actions and interactions. This shared reality is expired, as objectivity is factual and subjectively meaningful. In this sense, Berger and Luckmann wanted to deal in an integrated fashion with 'the dual character of society in terms of objective facticity and subjective meaning' (ibid.: 18). By subjective, they mean that reality is personally meaningful to the individual. By objective, they refer to the social order. This fact is clarified in Berger's book, *The Sacred Canopy*, in a more precise manner:

> Worlds are socially constructed and socially maintained. Their continuing reality, objective (as common, taken-for-granted facticity), and subjective (as facticity imposing itself on individual consciousness) depend upon specific social processes, namely those processes that continuously reconstruct and maintain the particular worlds in question. Conversely, the interruption of these social processes threatens the (objective and subjective) reality of the worlds in question. Thus, each world requires a social 'base' for its continuing existence as a real world to actual human beings (Berger, 1969: 45).

The primary thrust and essence of this phenomenological approach to social reality, according to them, is to integrate large and small-scale phenomena: *Society is a human product. Society is an objective reality. Man is a social product* (Berger and Luckmann, 1967: 61). In other words, people are the products of the very society that they create.

Berger and Luckmann wanted to study social reality in everyday life away from the study of intellectual history from the perspective of the sociology of knowledge. Here, we begin with an analysis of everyday life.

Everyday Life: The heart of this theory deals with the question of how everyday reality is socially constructed. As they put it, 'How is it possible that subjective meanings *become* objective facticities?' (ibid.: 18). They began their analysis at the individual level with the reality of everyday life, the commonsense world. Here, Berger and Luckmann seem to be influenced by the work of Alfred Schutz.

Berger and Luckmann's phenomenological analysis are focused on the view of how subjective processes become objective reality. In their opinion, people tend to apprehend everyday life as an ordered reality. In this sense, social reality seems independent of the actor's apprehension. It appears already objectified and seems to impose itself on the actor. This tendency leads to the objectification involved in language, which 'continuously provides (people) with the necessary objectification and posits the order within which these make sense and within which everyday life has meaning for (people)' (Berger and Luckmann, 1967: 23).

The reality of everyday life, therefore, should be taken for granted.

Berger and Luckmann are, like Goffman, convinced by the face-to-face interaction by which they include an individual in their sociology. Following Schutz's description of face-to-face interaction, they called *we-relationships.* They emphasized that such relationships involve an immediate interchange of meanings. In we-relationships, there is less typification, and it is more personalized than in they relationships. Their definition of social structure illustrates the importance of typification to Berger and Luckmann. They define social structure as 'The total of this typification and the recurrent patterns of interaction established by means of them' (ibid.: 23).

In addition, language is essential to Berger and Luckmann in the typification process. They viewed language as a specific form of the process of 'signification', a subtype of objectification. They accept the importance of language in social structure: 'I encounter language as a facticity external to myself and it is coercive on me' (ibid.: 38). Herer position on language seems to be very similar to Durkheimian understanding of social facts. However, Berger and Luckmann include both objectives and subjective reality in their framework, making it more than a purely micro-sociological approach. To clarify their phenomenological understanding, Berger and Luckmann put forward three concepts: *externalization, objectivation* and *internalization.*

1. *Externalization:* In externalization, individuals, with their human activity, create their social world. Berger and Luckmann view the social order as an ongoing human production. Thus, the social order is both the 'result of past human activity' and

'exists only as human activity continues to produce it' (Berger and Luckmann, 1967: 52). Thus, externalization has two dimensions. First, humans can create a new social reality, like forming friendships or starting a new business. Second, human beings can re-create social institutions through ongoing externalization, like maintaining and renewing old companies and old businesses or paying income tax. In the construction of social reality, people must externalize. In other words, people must do such things as produce what they need to survive and interact with others. In externalization, people are prone to develop habituated patterns of acting and interacting in recurrent situations. In the externalization phase of reality construction, Berger and Luckmann see individuals as creative beings capable of acting on their environment. In short, externalization means that individuals create society.

2. *Objectivation:* Objectivation is the process whereby individuals apprehend everyday life as an ordered, prearranged reality that imposes itself upon but is seemingly independent of human beings (Wallace and Wolf, 1980: 256). As Berger and Luckmann put it, 'The reality of everyday life appears already objectified, that is, constituted by order of objects that have been designated *as* objects before my appearance on the scene' (Berger and Luckmann, 1967: 22).

In the process of objectivation, language is used as a medium of construction of social reality.

> The common objectivations of everyday life are maintained primarily by linguistic signification. Everyday life is, above all, life with and using the language I share with my fellowmen. Thus, language is essential for understanding the reality of everyday life (ibid.: 37).

For example, the friendship between two people, which resulted from their interactions, confronts the two friends as a social reality is an example of objectivation. Other people can understand their friendship by hearing the language designating it. In short, objectivation means that society is an objective reality.

3. *Internalization:* Internalization is a kind of socialization by which the legitimation of the institutional order is assured. For Berger, successful socialization means a high degree of symmetry between objective and subjective reality and objective and

subjective identity (Wallace and Wolf, 1980: 257). Internalization for Berger is what socialization is for Parsons. In short, internalization means 'everyone pretty much *is* what he is supposed to be'. There is no problem with identity, for 'everybody knows who everybody is and who he is himself' (Berger and Luckmann, 1967: 164).

In addition, Berger's definition of socialization seems like Parsons': the internalization of social norms and values. However, Berger distinguishes between primary and secondary socialization. Primary socialization refers to what individuals undergo in childhood when they encounter significant others with whom they identify emotionally (Wallace and Wolf, 1980: 257).

'The child takes on the significant others' roles and attitudes, that is, internalizes them and makes them his own' (Berger and Luckmann, 1967: 131-2). Secondary socialization is 'any subsequent process that inducts an already socialized individual into new sectors of the objective world of his society' (ibid.: 130). Secondary socialization is a later phase in acquiring knowledge that occurs under the auspices of specialized agencies, like modern educational institutions.

The social construction of reality tries to bridge the gap between objective and subjective reality on the one hand and macro- and micro-level social theorizing on the other. It argues that individuals conform to existing social institutions' expectations whenever they engage in internalization and are *re-creating that social institution.* The creation of a new institution occurs in the moment of externalization; once externalized, it is objectified and once objectified, it acts back on the individual as an internalized entity. As Berger and Luckmann sum it up: 'Society is a human product' (Externalization), 'society is an objective reality' (Objectivation). 'Man is a social product' (Internalization) (ibid.: 61).

IV. CONCLUSION

Phenomenological sociology is sociology that operates based on philosophical phenomenology called transcendental phenomenology. It applies the principles of philosophical phenomenology to sociological questions. In this, the work of Dilthey, Rickert,

Windelband, Weber, Franz Brentano and Husserl provides its ultimate source in the development of the phenomenological sociology of Schutz and, Berger and Luckmann. Phenomenological sociologists give a more considerable degree of conceptual analysis from both the perspectives of macro and micro on the one hand and objective and subjective reality on the other. Schutzian phenomenology represents an abstract, theoretical and methodological orientation based on consciousness phenomena, meaning typification and lifeworld. Berger's theory of the social construction of reality is more like functionalism, which involves socialization as the internalization of societal values and norms. However, although Berger reminds us that the social order is a human product, he never addresses whether some people are better positioned to create social reality. At the same time, phenomenological sociologists are not careful in analysing taken-for-granted meanings when dealing with objective and subjective reality. However, these concepts for phenomenologists become a tool in the analysis. Phenomenological sociology provides a better platform for thinking about various social issues related to everyday life based on commonsense understanding. This approach is a radical alternative to the positivistic approach, which only emphasizes society. Therefore, phenomenology prefers considering individuals and social reality based on a particular situation. In short, phenomenological sociology is a science because of its rigorous, systematic and critical attempt to uncover the fundamental realities of social life.

KEY TERMS

Consciousness: According to Husserl, 'Consciousness itself has a being of its own which in its absolute uniqueness of nature remains unaffected by the phenomenological disconnection'.

Epistemology: The study or theory of knowledge, its origin, nature and limits.

Epoche: The *epoche* or bracketing eliminates any personal position or attitude relating to factual existence.

Externalization: It means that individuals create society. Berger and Luckmann have discussed it.

Folgewelt: It refers to denote the realm of successors. It is also one of the social world's realms, as Schutz discussed.

Ideographic: It describes unique events in their concreteness and individuality.

Institutionalization: Habitualized actions set the stage for the development of *institutionalization.* This occurs when people develop typification of what others are likely to do in each situation. Berger and Luckmann defined an *institution* as a reciprocal process of typification.

Intentionality: Brentano creates intentionality to distinguish between mental or psychological activities and physical phenomena.

Internalization: Internalization is a kind of socialization by which the legitimation of the institutional order is assured. Berger and Luckmann discussed this concept in their analysis of *The Social Construction of Reality.*

Lebenswelt: The *Lebenswelt* or lifeworld refers to the locus of reflective social action. The *Laben welt* is an intersubjective world. Lifeworld is concerned with pre-reflective experience in everyday life. It is also termed the 'world of the natural attitude'. This concept has been given by Husserl and discussed by Alfred Schutz.

Legitimations: Berger and Luckmann extensively treated *legitimations* as the explanations and justifications of the institutional system. Berger and Luckmann focused on the knowledge used to support their existence: 'Legitimation "explains" the institutional order by ascribing cognitive validity to its objectivated meaning. Legitimation justifies the institutional order by giving a normative dignity to its practical imperatives.' The focus is not on the structures being legitimated but on how they are legitimated.

Meanings: For Schutz, *meanings* concern how actors determine what aspects of the social world are essential.

Mitwelt: It refers to the realm of indirectly experienced social reality. It is the one type of social world, as discussed by Schutz.

Motives: For Schutz, *motives* involve the reason actors do what they do.

Nomothetic: It is used to uncover the general law of natural science.

Objectivation: It is the process whereby individuals apprehend everyday life as an ordered, prearranged reality that imposes itself upon but is seemingly independent of human beings. In *The Social Construction of Reality*, Berger and Luckmann discussed and analysed objectivation.

Phenomenology: A method in philosophy that begins with the individual and his own conscious experience and tries to avoid prior assumptions, prejudices and philosophical dogmas. Phenomenology thus examines phenomena as they are apprehended in their 'immediacy' by the social actor.

Psychologism: It is the basis of all human interpretations of helpful knowledge. Brentano has discussed psychologism and then Husserl.

Reification: Reification is the tendency to *perceive* human products as if they were something else, 'such as facts of nature, results of cosmic laws or manifestations of divine will'. In other words, people lose sight of the dialectical relationship between them and their products. In addition to Marx, it has also been discussed by Berger and Luckmann.

Roles: Berger and Luckmann's definition of roles resembles their sense of objective social reality. To them, roles typify actors' expectations in given social situations.

They-relations: They-relations are characterized by interaction with impersonal contemporaries rather than associates—Schutz's concepts of *mitwelt* fall into this category.

Transcendental ego: It pervades all acts and objects of consciousness, giving sense and validity to the world and constituting its meaning. The transcendental ego connects the subjectivity of perception to the objectivity of a universally accepted epistemology.

Transcendental phenomenology: It is dominated by Edmund Husserl's search for the essential foundations of knowledge in experience: an endeavour to formulate a basis for knowledge 'free from presuppositions'.

Typification: In typification, actors use their knowledge to categorize each other and adjust their responses to this typification; hence, actors can effectively deal with their world.

Umwelt: It refers to the realm of directly experienced social reality. Schutz has discussed it.

Vorwelt: It denotes the realm of predecessors. The realms of successors and predecessors (*Folgewelt* and *Vorwelt*) are of peripheral interest to Schutz.

We-relations: We-relations are defined by a relatively high degree of intimacy, determined by the extent to which the actors are acquainted with one another's biographies. The pure we-relationship is a face-to-face relationship.

REFERENCES

Abraham, M. Francis, *Modern Sociological Theory: An Introduction,* Calcutta: Oxford University Press, 2000.

Aron, Raymond, *German Sociology* (trans. Mary and Thomas Bottomore), New York: Free Press, 1967.

Berger, Peter L. and Thomas Luckmann, *The Social Construction of Reality,* New York: Doubleday and Co. Inc., 1967.

Berger, Peter L., *The Sacred Canopy,* New York: Doubleday and Co. Inc., 1969.

Dickens, David, 'Phenomenology', in Scott McNall (ed.), *Theoretical Perspectives in Sociology,* New York: St. Martin's Press, 1979.

Gorman, Robert A., 'Phenomenology and Methodology of Social Science: The Origins', in *The Classical Tradition in Sociology: The European Tradition,* Raymond Boudon, Mohamed Cherkaoui and Jeffrey Alexander (eds.), vol. III, London: Sage Publications, 1997.

Husserl, Edmund, *Ideas: General Introduction to Pure Phenomenology* (trans. W.R. Boyce Gibson), New York: Humanities Press, 1931.

Mitchel, G. Duncan (ed.), *A New Dictionary of Sociology,* London: Routledge, 1999.

Ritzer, George, *Sociological Theory,* Singapore: McGraw Hill Publishing Company, 1988.

Schutz, Alfred, *Collected Papers,* vol. I, edited by Maurice Natanson and Martinus Mijhoff, The Hague, 1962.

——, *The Phenomenology of the Social World,* Northwestern University Press, Evanston, (1932) 1967.

Turner, Jonathan H., *The Structure of Sociological Theory,* Homewood: The Dorsey Press, 1978.

Wallace, Ruth A. and Alison Wolf, *Contemporary Sociological Theory: Continuing the Classical Tradition,* Englewood Cliffs: Prentice-Hall, Inc., 1980.

Weber, Max, *The Methodology of the Social Sciences* (trans. and ed. Edward A. Shills and Henry A. Finch), Chicago: Free Press, 1949.

CHAPTER 4

Ethnomethodology

Ethnomethodology is the most recent theoretical and methodological perspective in sociology. The term *ethnomethodology* is the study of methods used by the common people of society in everyday activity. The central concern of ethnomethodology 'is to demonstrate how society is the ongoing practical accomplishment of rational individuals' (Weigert, 1981: 38).

The term was coined by the American sociologist Harold Garfinkel, who is generally regarded as its founder. Garfinkel discusses *ethnomethodology* in his book *Studies in Ethnomethodology*, published in 1967. Heritage defined *ethnomethodology* as the study of 'The body of commonsense knowledge and the range of procedures and considerations by means of which the ordinary members of society make sense of finding their way about it and act on the circumstances in which they find themselves' (Heritage, 1984: 4).

Ethnomethodology has its roots in phenomenology and symbolic interactionism. Here, one central question related to ethnomethodology development is: what should sociologists' study? For the ethnomethodologist,

> What is directly observable are people's efforts to create a commonsense of social reality. The substance of this reality is viewed as less interesting than the *methods* used by groups of persons, whether sociologists or laypersons, to construct, reaffirm and alter a vision and image of what exists 'out there' (Turner J., 1978: 405).

In this sense, the 'methodology' used in the ethnomethodological investigation does not address a question about the 'proper', 'unbiased' or 'truly scientific' search for knowledge. Ethnomethodology is mainly concerned with the standard methods used by people whether they are scientists, housewives, salespersons or labourers—to create a sense of order in the situations in which they interact. The best way to understand it is in the word 'ethnomethodology' itself—an *Ethno* means 'folk or people' the methods (used by), and *ology,* 'study of method'.

Ethnomethodologists have extended the concerns of symbolic interactionism and phenomenology and focused on microscopic aspects of human behaviour. Ethnomethodologists have borrowed the idea of symbolic interactionism in how actors create common meanings in dealing with each other in the interaction process. Blumer, an interactionist, rightly points out, 'It would be wise to recognize that any given (act) is mediated by acting units interpreting the situations with which they are confronted' (Blumer, 1962).

In other words, actors are capable of (a) introjecting new objects into situations, (b) redefining situations, and (c) rearranging their joint actions. These ideas concern how meanings or definitions are created by actors interacting in situations. Ethnomethodologists also emphasize this line of inquiry by focusing on interaction and the creation of meanings in situations. Turner (1978: 406) points out a significant shift in emphasis: In what ways do people create a *sense* that they share a common view of the world? And how do people arrive at the *presumption* that there is an objective, external world? Blumer's interactionism stresses the process of creating meaning, but it acknowledges the existence of an external social order. Ethnomethodology suspends the issue of whether there is an external world of norms, roles, values and beliefs. Instead, it concentrates on how interaction creates a sense of a real-world 'out there' among actors.

On the other hand, Ethnomethodologists have borrowed the idea of commonsense reality constructed in everyday interaction. However, the ethnomethodologists' position is different from the phenomenologists in that they (ethnomethodologists) emphasize the process by which commonsense reality is constructed in everyday face-to-face interaction. However, Schutz strongly influenced Harold Garfinkel, the founder of ethnomethodology, who sought to understand the methods employed by people to make sense of their world.

The primary purposes of ethnomethodological investigation are: (1) to study a particular situation of society from the methods used by ordinary people, and (2) to study a neglected phenomenon of the world of daily life. Hence, ethnomethodology proposes studying both topics and determining how they acquire their mundane, commonplace, commonly known character.

I. HAROLD GARFINKEL (1917-2011)

Harold Garfinkel is recognized as the leading figure, founder, and father of ethnomethodology. He was born on 29 October 1917 and died on 21 April 2011. He completed his PhD at Harvard University in 1952, aside from two years of teaching at Ohio State University and a brief interim on a research project at the University of Chicago. He taught at the University of California in Los Angeles. He did not produce a single major work but has had many of his best articles published in a collected volume entitled *Studies in Ethnomethodology,* published in 1967. Garfinkel is indebted to four persons whose writing have provided him with in-exhaustible directives toward the world of everyday activities. They are Talcott Parsons, under whom he studied at Harvard; Alfred Schutz, whom he visited and studied under at the New School for Social Research; and the phenomenological philosophers Aron Gurwitch and Edmund Husserl.

Garfinkel has established an ethnomethodological approach based on his analysis of tapes of jury deliberations conducted in 1945. The term 'ethnomethodology' was coined when Garfinkel worked with their cross-cultural files at Yale. During this time, he came upon the files card entitled 'ethnobotany, ethnophysiology, ethnophysics'. He became interested in 'how the jurors knew what they were doing in doing the work of jurors' (Wallace and Wolf, 1980: 238). In the jury deliberation project, he came to know the methodology that jurors used and decided to name this method *ethnomethodology.* 'He created "ethnomethodology"', explains Roy Turner, "because ethno" refers to the availability to a member of commonsense knowledge of his society as commonsense knowledge of the "whatever"' (Turner, R., 1974: 16).

Thus, ethnomethodology studies 'folk' or commonsense methods employed by people to make sense of everyday activities by constructing and maintaining social reality. Therefore, ethnomethodology is interested in how people make sense of everyday activities. In short, Garfinkel's ethnomethodology can be outlined in the following points:

(*i*) It studies members' methods of making sense of their social world.

(*ii*) It examines the methods by which people do this. People create an actual world by 'making sense' of events in terms of a preconceived order for society.

(*iii*) It sees the objective reality of social facts as an 'ongoing accomplishment of the concerted activities of everyday life' (Garfinkel, 1967: vii). In other words, in everyday situations, individuals invoke or recognize social facts, such as taken-for-granted norms or values, that interpret the meaning of the situation for them.

(*iv*) Ethnomethodological studies 'analyse everyday activities as members' methods for making those same activities visibly-rational-and-reportable-for-all-practical-purposes, that is, 'accountable' as organizations of commonplace every day activities' (ibid.).

(*v*) It studies the process by which people invoke specific taken-for-granted rules about behaviour with which they interpret an interaction situation and make it meaningful. In ethnomethodology, the interpretive process is a phenomenon for investigation (Wallace and Wolf, 1980: 240).

(*vi*) It answers how, but not why, about social interaction, while the other micro-sociological theories answer why but not how. 'Ethnomethodologists cannot study social processes that transcend interaction while the other micro-sociological theories cannot address the formal structure of practical knowledge within interaction' (Handel, 1993: 193-4).

Ethnomethodological investigation consists of various concepts. The core concepts are: (1) Reflexivity, (2) Indexicality, (3) Sanctioned properties of common discourse, and (4) Sense in a senseless situation.

1. *Reflexivity:* Reflexivity focuses on how people in interaction maintain the presumption that a particular reality guides them (Turner, J., 1978: 411). A reflexive action, therefore, is an action the acting agent takes upon itself. For example, when I share myself, the action is reflexive. In a broader sense, a reflexive action operates to maintain a particular vision of reality. For example, ritual activity is directed toward the gods in the belief that gods influence everyday affairs. Much human interaction is reflexive. 'Humans interpret cues, gestures, words and other information from each other in a way that sustains a particular vision of reality. Contradictional evidence is reflexively interpreted to maintain a body of belief and knowledge' (ibid.: 411).

   Ethnomethodological inquiry addresses the concepts and principles in explaining the conditions under which different reflexive actions among interacting parties are likely to occur.
2. *Indexicality:* Indexicality refers to understanding a particular situation based on contextual reality. In this sense, the gestures, cues, words and other information sent and received by interacting parties have meaning in a *particular context* (ibid.). Without knowing the context, it would be possible to misinterpret the symbolic communication among interacting individuals. In other words, the practical sociological reasoning of ethnomethodological inquiry is based on the indexical properties of members' talk and conduct. Garfinkel uses ethnomethodology to investigate the rational properties of indexical expression and other practical actions.
3. *Sanctioned Properties of Common Discourse:* This refers to people's expectation that there will be no interference with everyday affairs in the form of questions about what is 'reality said' (Wallace and Wolf, 1980: 243). In other words, it is expected and required that people understand everyday talk in the same way that it is so that common conversational affairs can be conducted without interference. To illustrate this property, we can cite Garfinkel's experiment: 'Students were instructed to engage an acquaintance or a friend in an ordinary conversation and, without indicating that what the experimenter was asking

was in any way unusual, to insist that the person clarify the sense of his commonplace remarks' (Garfinkel, 1967: 42).

4. *Sense in a Senseless Situation:* Garfinkel attempted to demonstrate that sense could be made in a senseless environment and that when subjects abandoned belief in the understanding of the environment, they could perceive how the environment was given sense in the first place. To demonstrate that sense could be made in a senseless environment, Garfinkel produced a partly senseless environment in the laboratory (Handel, 1993: 200). In one of the demonstrations, students were told to act as 'boarders' in their homes.

Having discussed four characteristics involved in the ethnomethodological inquiry, we find two key concepts, reflexivity and indexicality, are central to this approach. Here, the emphasis is not on the context of the 'lifeworld' but on the methods or techniques that actors use to create, maintain or even alter a vision of reality. As Mehan and Wood say, 'The ethnomethodological theory of the reality constructor is about the *procedures* that accomplish reality. It is not about any specific reality' (Mehan and Wood, 1975: 114).

This emphasis led to the isolation by ethnomethodologists of general types of methods employed by interacting actors.

GENERAL INTERACTIVE METHODS

Before going into details about the methods used in an ethnomethodological investigation, we focus on people's general techniques to construct their reality. Aaron Cicourel has summarized several techniques or methods isolated by ethnomethodologists: (1) searching for the normal form, (2) doing reciprocity of perspectives, and (3) using the et cetera principle (Cicourel, 1973: 85-8).

1. *Searching for the normal form:* It is explained by Turner as, 'If interacting parties' sense that ambiguity exists over what is real and that their interaction is thus difficult, they will emit gestures to tell each other to return to what is "normal" in their contextual situations' (Turner, J., 1967: 412).

In this sense, actors should try to maintain a normal form of interacting with situations.

2. *Doing reciprocity of perspectives:* Borrowing from Schutz's formulation,

> ethnomethodologists have emphasized that actors operate under the presumption and actively seek to communicate the fact that they would have the same experiences were they to switch places and that until so informed by specific gestures, they can each ignore differences in perspectives which might arise from their unique biographies (Turner, J., 1967: 412).

Thus, the gesture interaction would assure others that perspective reciprocity exists.

3. *Using the et cetera principle:* Much is left 'unsaid' when examining an actual interaction. Actors must constantly 'fill in' or 'wait for' information necessary to 'make sense' of another's words or deeds (ibid.: 412). Garfinkel refers to 'filling in' the meanings to talk as the 'et cetera' principle. It is a 'shorthand' way of speaking. For example, Garfinkel gives an assignment to his students to 'Report common conversations by writing on the left side of a sheet what the parties actually said and on the right side what they and their partners (in the conversation) understand that they were talking about' (ibid.: 38).

The result is that much more is written on the right-hand side than on the left. What is 'left out' on the left-hand side is related (as Garfinkel puts it) to 'The previous course of the conversation or the particular relationship of actual or potential interaction that exists between user and auditor' (ibid.: 40).

Thus, the et cetera principle is used to get needed information without disrupting the interaction and reality.

These three generals' 'folk methods' refer to what ethnomethodologists seek to discover. In addition to these folk methods, ethnomethodologists also use other detailed methods. The goal of ethnomethodology is to determine the conditions under which these and other interpersonal techniques will be used to construct, maintain or change a reality. These methods are: (a) the Breaching experiment, and (b) the Documentary method.

(a) *Breaching experiment:* Garfinkel and his associates conducted many interesting empirical studies to understand their assumptions about 'what is real'. For this, they used a method for empirical inquiry known as the 'breaching experiment', in which the researchers deliberately interrupt the ordinary course of interaction. Garfinkel has not recognized an actual experiment in the formal sense of the term and might better be called a 'breaching demonstration' (Ritzer, 1988: 358). Social reality is 'breached' in this demonstration to demonstrate the basic principles of ongoing reality construction. 'The objective of the breaching experiment is to disrupt normal procedures so that the process by which reality is constructed or reconstructed can be observed' (ibid.: 358).

A breaching experiment is undertaken to illustrate how people make sense of their everyday lives. However, the reactions to breaches are sometimes so extreme that Hugh Mehan and Wood have cautioned about their use: 'Interested persons are strongly advised not to undertake any new breaching studies' (Mehan and Wood, 1975: 113).

(b) *Documentary method:* Another important method used by sociologists who are 'doing ethnomethodology' is called the 'documentary method of interpretation'. Garfinkel credits Mannheim with the label and quotes his definition as the search for 'an identical homologous pattern underlying a wide variety of totally different realizations of meaning'. Garfinkel says:

> The method consists of treating an actual appearance as 'the document of', as 'pointing to' and as 'standing on behalf of' a presupposed underlying pattern. Not only is the underlying pattern derived from its documentary evidence, but the individual documentary evidence, in turn, is interpreted based on 'what is known' about the underlying pattern (Garfinkel, 1967: 78).

In other words, both laypeople and sociologists use the documentary method, which involves an effort to identify. 'an *underlying pattern* behind a series of appearances such that each appearance is seen as referring to, an expression of or a document of, the underlying pattern' (Wilson, 1970: 68).

To Garfinkel, the documentary method is constantly used by people to interpret and reinterpret each other's behaviour and look for underlying patterns.

In short, Garfinkel's ethnomethodology emphasizes members' methods rather than members of society. The ethnomethodologist asks about how such meanings are 'locally' managed and how members in the setting accomplish the here-and-there practical relevance of their understandings. It can be said that ethnomethodological studies end at the point where symbolic interactionist studies *begin.* The ethnomethodologist speaks of the 'local production' of experiences and the methods by which members 'assemble the sense' of situational particulars. In this sense, Garfinkel's idea of ethnomethodology is better known for practical sociological reasoning that emphasizes the inquiry of a particular situation.

II. ERVING GOFFMAN (1922-1982)

Goffman was born in Alberta, Canada, on 11 June 1922. He did his PhD at the University of Chicago. He is usually considered a symbolic interactionist and belongs to the Chicago school of thought. However, Goffman represents a significant source of inspiration for ethnomethodology. Goffman's work has often been termed the 'dramaturgical school' of interactionism because it focuses on how an actor manipulates gestures to create an impression in a particular social scene. Goffman's idea of the dramaturgical approach is mainly related to the process of impression management. As Turner puts it, 'Goffman has insightfully analysed how actors validate self-conceptions, justify their actions through gestures, demonstrate their membership in groups, display social distance and adjust to physical stigmas and how they interpersonally manipulate many other situations' (Turner, J., 1967: 406).

Goffman is best known for his dramaturgical approach, which appeared in his magnum opus, *The Presentation of Self in Everyday Life,* published in 1959. However, Goffman produced a significant body of work before publishing *The Presentation of Self.* In his early work, his main emphasis was on two broad accounts of face-to-face interaction: one emphasizes manipulation and impression management; the other highlights the importance of ritual and tactful accommodation (Manning, Phil, 1997: 285).

The Presentation of Self in Everyday Life was first published by the University of Edinburgh in 1959 and was later expanded for a second edition published simultaneously in Great Britain and the United States. The later version contains some changes: it is divided into more paragraphs and the word 'one' is substituted for 'we'. There are also important additions—a new section to the 'Performances' chapter and an extension to the conclusion. Goffman describes *The Presentation of Self* as 'a sort of handbook', a 'report' outlining six dramaturgical 'principles'. Here, he takes the dramatic situation of actors and actresses on stage and applies this theatrical representation to the simple lines of ordinary women and men acting out their roles in the real world (Wallace and Wolf, 1980: 224). The six principles of the dramaturgical approach are performance, the team, the region, discrepant roles, communication out of character and impression management.

Goffman defines a performance as 'all the activity of a given participant on a given occasion which serves to influence in any way of the other participants' (Goffman, 1959: 26). He again adds,

> I have been using the term 'performance' to refer to all the activity of an individual which occurs during a period marked by his continuous presence before a particular set of observers and which has some influence on the observers (ibid.: 32).

There is a front region in all social interaction, which parallels the stage front in a theatrical performance. Actors on the stage and in social life are seen as being interested in appearances, wearing costumes and using props. During the performance, actors perform their actions based on the occasion's needs so that the performance would appear more attractive.

Successful performance on the stage is always done by a group of people called 'teams'. Teams perform in 'front regions', spaces from which they are observable by their different publics. Another region type is a 'back region', where the actors can retire to prepare themselves for their performance. In theatre, the actors can shed their roles and be themselves backstage or offstage. Throughout this discussion, Goffman avoids the claim that authenticity can be regionalized; instead, he suggests that locations affect our perceptions of behaviour in misinformed ways (Manning, Phil, 1997: 287).

Team performances' regional behaviour (front and backstage) provides performers with a secret to keep. 'When knowledge of back-region activities could be of value, various people with "discrepant roles" attempt to gain access by masquerading as team members' (ibid.).

Whether the region is front or back, they aim to discover the different types of secrets held by team members during the performance.

The information provides performers to perform their activities in the right direction. Their failure to do that is often acknowledged without bursts such as 'Oh God!' It all happens when performers disclose damaging facts inadvertently. Fearing the disclosure of discreditable information encourages performers to practice the art of impression management and to avoid unpleasant 'scenes' in which everyone's *projected* self may become irreconcilable with the *presented* self (Goffman, 1959: 206). Impression management is oriented toward guarding against unexpected actions, such as unintended gestures, inopportune intrusions, etc. However, Ritzer points out successful impression management from the audience's point of view. In his words,

> The audience also has a stake in successful impression management by the actor or team of actors. The audience often acts to save the show through such devices as giving great interest and attention to it, avoiding emotional outbursts, not noticing slips and giving special consideration to a neophyte performer (Ritzer, 1988: 310).

The six theatrical principles of *The Presentation of Self* can be used to interpret everyday behaviour. However, Goffman has indicated a methodological problem: how to make the socially organized features of interactional behaviour visible and describable. He provides a solution using analytic metaphors. He uses the metaphor of the theatrical performance to describe aspects of self-presentation in daily life. On stage, the actor presents himself to the audience as a particular character in the play. He must make them aware that he is a policeman or a king through costume, props, scenery and movement and the dialogue written for him. During his achievement of the character, he is supported not only by the other actors on the stage but also by those who work behind the scenes, such as the make-up staff, scene-changers, director and so on. All these parties are involved in staging the play and projecting the characters' identities to the audience.

In some respects, the individual in everyday situations can be seen as having the same problem as the stage actor. When we enter a setting or occasion, we communicate to others who and what we are. The only way others can judge what type or kind of person we are is through our conduct and appearance. Another essential element of the presentation of self in everyday settings, as discussed by Goffman, is teamwork. For example, a hospital's staff can be seen as a team seeking to sustain for patients and their relatives the conviction that competent and effective medical work is being done on their behalf. This effective effort is often the outcome of the behaviour of many people.

In short, Goffman's works are straightforward to read, but it is difficult to grasp his point. He deals with the minutiae of social life and face-to-face interaction in a theatrical setting. Most importantly, he analysed everything based on empirical materials. Here, he draws his fieldwork or that of other researchers, but interspersed with these sociological sources are references to unconventional materials, such as novels, biographies and memoirs, books of etiquette, rule books, instruction manuals, newspaper cuttings and so forth. Goffman's analysis of the management of social scenes is also prominent in the ethnomethodological approach. Ethnomethodologists share Goffman's concern with the techniques by which actors create impressions in social situations. Still, their interest is not in individuals' impression management but in how actors create a *sense* of a common reality. Ethnomethodologists, however, concentrate on interaction techniques, but they ask a somewhat different question than Goffman.

GOFFMAN'S INTERACTION ORDER

'The Interaction Order' is the final work of Goffman, which was published in the *American Sociological Review.* In this work, Goffman focuses on face-to-face interaction, 'where two or more individuals are physically in one another's presence' (Goffman, 1983: 8). The organization of interaction arises mainly from the *interactional* circumstances with the range of one another's observation and communication. Goffman's work has shown that the organization of social interaction can be studied as a phenomenon. He outlines some of the basic units and recurrent structures and processes of the interaction order, from the smallest to the largest: (1) *persons,* whether single, couples, files, processions or queues; (2) *contacts,* either through physical co-presence, telephone conversation or letter exchange; (3) *encounters* or arrangements in which persons come together into a small physical circle as participants in a consciously shared, interdependent undertaking (for example, card games, meals, lovemaking and service transactions); (4) *platform performances,* where activity is set before an audience (for instance, a talk, a contest, a formal meeting, a play, a musical offering); and (5) *celebrative social occasions,* gatherings of individuals in honour of some jointly appreciated circumstances where participants arrive and leave in a coordinated way (Wallace and Wolf, 1980: 228). The last unit is the most significant interactional order by which individuals can interact over many days.

Although the persons, contacts, encounters, performances and celebrations outlined above are microscopic, Goffman argues that the interaction order directly affects the macroscopic order. Goffman states that a good deal of organizational work is done through face-to-face interaction. For example, complex organizations depend on particular personnel, especially those in governing roles, so they are highly vulnerable when key personnel are abducted or injured. In this article, Goffman attempted to synthesize symbolic interactionism by focusing on Simmel's view about the interaction order, which consists of persons, contacts, encounters, platform performances and celebrations. Goffman also claims that forms of face-to-face life are more open to systematic analysis than many macroscopic entities. His central theme of symbolic interactionism is: 'That actor interprets, maps out, evaluates and then acts; that is, that human beings are active, not passive' (ibid.: 229).

Goffman's legacy in sociology emerges as advocating a new direction for research on the interaction order.

KEY TERMS

Accounts: Accounting is the process by which people make sense of the world (Handel, 1982: 24). Accounts are how actors do such things as describe, analyse, criticize and idealize specific situations. Ethnomethodologists devote a lot of attention to exploring people's accounts as well as to how accounts are offered and accepted (or rejected) by others.

Back region: The back region is the place close to and hidden from the audience where impression management techniques are practiced.

Breaching experiment: A breaching experiment is used to disrupt normal procedures so that the process by which reality is constructed or reconstructed can be observed. Garfinkel discusses it.

Conversation analysis: A significant part of ethnomethodology is *conversation analysis.* The 'description and explication of the competencies that ordinary speakers use and rely on in participating in intelligible, socially organized interaction', or 'the procedures by which conversationalists produce their behaviour and understand and deal with the behaviour of others' (Heritage and Atkinson, 1984: 1). Conversation analysis look for the order, the regularities produced by and found in peoples' conversations.

Documentary method: Both laypeople and sociologists use the documentary method, which involves an effort to identify 'an underlying pattern behind a series of appearances such that each appearance is seen as referring to, an expression of or a document of the underlying pattern' (T. Wilson, 1970: 68).

Dramaturgy: Webster defines dramaturgy as 'the art of dramatic composition and theatrical representation' (Erving Goffman).

Et cetera principle: All situations involve incomplete aspects that the participants must fill in. In each case, we allow unclear information to pass on the assumption that it will be clarified later.

Ethnomethodology: It is the study of 'the body of commonsense knowledge and the range of procedures and considerations by means of which the ordinary members of society make sense of, find their way about in and act on the circumstances in which they find themselves' (Heritage, 1984: 4).

Front: The front is 'that part of the individual's performance which regularly functions in a general and fixed fashion to define the situation for those who observe the performance' (Erving Goffman).

Front region: The front region is where the actor is seriously playing out the script of impression management. Goffman has discussed it in theatrical performance.

Impression management: It is oriented to guarding against unexpected actions, such as unintended gestures, inopportune intrusion and so on.

Indexicality: Indexicality is derived from linguistics, describing the property of sentences to have different meanings in different contexts. Ethnomethodologists adopt the view that all accounts, all expressions and all practical actions must be interpreted within their context.

Natural language: This system of practices allows people to speak, hear and witness the objective production and display of social life. Natural language is concerned with the basic structure of speaker-hearer interaction.

Role distance: The degree to which an individual embraces a given role is called role distance. In his view, only some people get involved in any given role because of the many roles. Role distance, therefore, deals with the degree to which individuals separate themselves from their roles.

REFERENCES

Blumer, Herbert, 'Society as Symbolic Interaction', in A. Rose, ed., *Human Behaviour and Social Processes*, Boston: Houghton Mifflin, 1962.

Cicourel, Aron V., *Cognitive Sociology*, London: Macmillan, 1973.

Garfinkel, Harold, *Studies in Ethnomethodology*, Englewood Cliffs: Prentice-Hall, Inc., 1967.

——, 'The Interaction Order', *American Sociological Review*, 48, February 1983.

——, *The Presentation of Self in Everyday Life*, 2nd edn., Harmondsworth: Penguin, 1959.

Handel, Warren H., *Contemporary Sociological Theory*, Englewood Cliffs: Prentice-Hall, Inc., , 1993.

Heritage, John, *Garfinkel and Ethnomethodology*, Cambridge: Polity Press, 1984.

Manning, Phil, 'Drama as Life: The Significance of Goffman's Changing Use of the Theatrical Metaphor', In Jeffrey Alexander, Raymond Boudon and Mohamed Cherkaoui (eds.), *The Classical Tradition in Sociology: The American Tradition*, vol. IV, London: Sage Publications, 1997.

Mehan, Hugh and Houston Wood, *The Reality of Ethnomethodology*, New York: Wiley, 1975.

Ritzer, George, *Sociological Theory*, Singapore: McGraw-Hill Publishing Company, 1988.

Turner, Jonathan H., *The Structure of Sociological Theory*, Homewood: The Dorsey Press, 1978.

Turner, Roy, ed., *Ethnomethodology: Selected Readings*, Baltimore: Penguin Books, 1974.

Wallace, Ruth A. and Alison Wolf, *Contemporary Sociological Theory: Continuing the Classical Tradition*, Englewood Cliffs: Prentice-Hall, Inc., 1980.

Weigert, Andrew, *Sociology of Everyday Life*, New York: Longman, , 1981.

Wilson, Thomas P., 'Normative and Interpretive Paradigms in Sociology', In Jack Douglas (ed.), *Understanding Everyday Life*, Chicago: Aldine, 1970.

CHAPTER 5

Neo-Functionalism

Neo-functionalism is a recent development in contemporary sociological theory. It is considered a discovery and reconstruction of Parson's functionalism. At the beginning of the 1960s, functionalism started to decline its theoretical position in sociology. It is clear from the statement that Kingsley Davis made in 1959. In his article, Davis argued that 'a functionalist does not have to believe that everything that exists meets a need, is indispensable or is in a system where all the parts work for the good of the whole. The functionalist must conclude that things are interrelated, and that society is integrated or 'working (functioning) most of the time'. In this sense, the functionalist approach for sociologists is most important. But specific problems existed in the functional approach, so it was necessary to reconstruct it.

This needs to reconstruct the functionalist school of sociology that gave birth to the neo-functional approach. However, neo-functionalists took various concepts from Parsons's functional approach, but they also rejected some of his analyses. Jeffrey C. Alexander and Paul Colomy are some of the famous and pioneer contributors of neo-functionalism. They did not consider neo-functionalism as a developed theory rather than a tendency. This section will discuss Alexander's analysis of neo-functionalism and his view on multidimensional sociology.

JEFFREY C. ALEXANDER (1947-)

Jeffrey C. Alexander is one of America's prominent social theorists, born in 1947. *Theoretical Logic in Sociology* is considered his first major publication. He is known for his neo-functional approach in social sciences in general and sociology in particular. Alexander's neo-functionalism emphasized the linkages between macro- and micro-levels of analysis and reconceptualized core elements of the functionalist approach to sociology. His neo-functional analysis is based on the criticisms and reconstruction of Parsons's approach.

I. ALEXANDER'S NEO-FUNCTIONALISM

Neo-functionalism has been discussed considering the declining significance of structural functionalism from the mid-1960s through the early 1980s. However, by the mid-1980s, a significant effort was underway to revive the theory under 'neo-functionalism'. This 'neo-functionalism' accepts many of the criticisms but provides an attempt to naturalize Talcott Parsons's general approach. Neo-functionalism was used to indicate continuity with structural functionalism and demonstrate that an effort was being made to extend structural functionalism and overcome its significant difficulties. Jeffrey Alexander and Paul Colomy define *neo-functionalism* as: 'A self-critical strand of a functional theory that seeks to broaden functionalism's intellectual scope while retaining its theoretical core' (Alexander and Colomy, 1985: 11).

Thus, it seems clear that Alexander and Colomy see structural functionalism as overly narrow and that their goal is to create a more synthetic theory. Orru concludes by suggesting that: 'the revival of Parsonian thought is one of the distinguishing features of 1980s sociology' (Orru, 1953 115-17).

Neo-functionalism appears to be the only new theoretical movement to have emerged in Western Sociology in the 1980s.

Before we turn to the discussion of neo-functionalism, it should be noted that functionalists emphasize cultural matters, agreement and differences in ideas and do not recognize the extent to which social relations are rooted in economic and political considerations. However, Parsons, throughout his intellectual life, sought to integrate a wide range of theoretical inputs and tried to interrelate the significant domains of the social world, most notably the cultural, social and personality systems. Here, we can say that Parsons adopted a narrow structural-functionalist orientation and saw the cultural system as determining the other systems. Thus, Parsons abandoned his synthetic orientation and neo-functionalism, it can be viewed as an effort to recapture such an orientation.

Alexander emphasizes the heuristic or exploratory nature of strategy and a willingness to accommodate other orientations in sociology. He has enumerated the problems associated with structural functionalism that neo-functionalism needs to surmount, including 'anti-individualism', 'antagonism to change', 'conservatism', 'idealism' and an 'anti-empirical bias' (Alexander, 1985: 10). Efforts were made to overcome these problems programmatically and give a new direction to the sociological approach in terms of neo-functionalism. Despite his enthusiasm for neo-functionalism, in the mid-1980s, Alexander was forced to conclude that: 'neo-functionalism is a tendency rather than a developed theory' (ibid.: 16).

In this context, Alexander admits that he has a long way to go to establish 'new' structural functionalism.

Although neo-functionalism may not be a development theory, however, Alexander (1985) has outlined some of its basic orientations:

(*i*) *Descriptive model of society:* Neo-functionalism provides a descriptive portrayal of society as a relatively self-contained system organized through the interaction of its parts which form a pattern. This pattern allows the system to be differentiated from its environment. Parts of the system are symbiotically oriented, and some overarching face does not determine their interaction (Ritzer, 1988: 255). Thus, neo-functionalism rejects any monocausal determinism discussed by the functionalist and is open-ended and pluralistic.

(*ii*) *Equilibrium and integration:* The ideas of system equilibrium and system integration are used as analytical tools to describe features of society. There is a concern for equilibrium within neo-functionalism, but it is broader than the structural-functional concern encompassing both moving and partial equilibrium (ibid.: 226). Equilibrium is seen as a reference point for functional analysis rather than as descriptive of the lives of individuals in actual systems. In this sense, there is a decline in seeing social systems as characterized by static equilibrium. On the other, Alexander states that integration is a possibility, and that deviance and social control are facts, thereby making quite clear that there is no naive assumption that actual societies are fully integrated.

(*iii*) *Equal attention to action and order:* Alexander argues that neo-functionalism gives equal attention to action and order. Thus, it avoids the tendency of structural functionalism to focus almost exclusively on the macro-level sources of order in social structure and culture and to give attention to more micro-level action patterns (ibid.: 225). Neo-functionalism devotes attention to all forms of action, including rational and expressive action.

(*iv*) *Acceptance of Parsonian Functionalism:* Neo-functionalism accepts the traditional Parsonian emphasis on personality, culture and social system. The interpenetration of culture, personality and social system is an essential feature of the mode of analysis of neo-functionalism and integration of these is a necessary feature of reality. A concern with the interaction of institutions in providing for the social system integration, functionalism must also analyse the organization of the culture and the socialization processes. Naive assumptions about the extent of integration *within* culture, personality and social system, as well as between them, must be avoided. Integration is not automatic or unproblematic; it produces tension that creates strain and provokes change.

(*v*) *Social change:* Neo-functionalism focuses on social change in the differentiation processes within the social, cultural and personality systems. Thus, change is not productive of conformity and harmony but rather 'individuation and institutional strains' (Alexander, 1985: 10). In this way, social change is not only a product of strain and tension but also produces strain and stress. However, Alexander accepts that these changes have moved society from one *relatively* integrated level to another and have become reintegrated at a higher level of adaptability.

(*vi*) *Independency in theorizing*: Alexander argues that neo-functionalism 'Implies the commitment to the independence of conceptualization and theorizing from other levels of sociological analysis' (ibid.: 10).

Alexander has tried to integrate Marx's work on material structures, Durkheim's on symbolism and Parsons's on structural functionalism into neo-functionalism. To overcome the idealist bias of Parsonian structural functionalism, especially its emphasis on macro-subjective phenomena like culture, more materialist approaches were encouraged. To eliminate the macro-level biases of traditional structural functionality, efforts were made to integrate ideas from exchange theory, symbolic interactionism, pragmatism, phenomenology and so on. In other words, Alexander and Colomy endeavoured to synthesize structural functionalism with many different theoretical traditions. Such a reconstruction could both revive structural functionalism and provide the base for developing a new theoretical tradition.

However, Alexander regards the neo-functionalist project as completed, and he is ready to move beyond not only to Parsons but also to neo-functionalism. In 'the New Theoretical Movement', Alexander believes that this theoretical perspective would be even more synthetic than neo-functionalism, drawing upon a wide range of academic resources. Alexander is seeking to do much more with micro-sociological and cultural theory developments.

II. ALEXANDER'S MULTIDIMENSIONAL SOCIOLOGY

In the first volume of his major work, *Theoretical Logic in Sociology*, Jeffrey Alexander seeks a 'new "theoretical logic" for sociology' (ibid.: xv). That new logic affects 'sociological thought at every level of the intellectual continuum' (ibid.: 65). Alexander tries to establish a multidimensional sociology involving an 'alternation of freedom and constraint' (ibid.: 74). Multidimensionality is the best-known expression of his synthesis. Multidimensionality involves two general propositions. The first consists of the problem of *action* or 'the particular nature of norms and motivation' (ibid.: 70).

Here, Alexander emphasizes that rational adaptations shape action to external conditions *and* actors' subjective commitments and perceptions. The second is the problem of *order* or 'how a plurality of such actions became interrelated and ordered' (ibid.: 90).

The order problem, according to Alexander, is mainly based on a macro-micro problem. Alexander suggests that there is a macro-micro continuum in terms of an 'individual' or 'collective' level of analysis of how an order is created in society (ibid.: 93). At the macro end of the continuum, the order is externally created and is collectivist. At the micro end, the order is derived from internalized forces and is individualistic. In a multi-dimensional framework, a collectivist concept of order is preferred, though individualistic theories' accounts of empirical processes are recognized as crucial to a comprehensive understanding of social life.

On the other hand, the action problem involves a materialist-idealist continuum that also implies a macro-micro dimension.

> At the idealist (subjective) end, action is described as normative (implying macro subjectivity), nonrational and effective. At the materialist (objective) end, action is instrumental (implying micro-objectivity), rational and conditional (Ritzer, 1988: 491).

In a multidimensional framework, then, the rational and non-rational determinants of action are given roughly equal analytical weight. In this sense, Alexander attempted to bridge the gap between macro and micro theorizing on the one hand and to relate between action and order on the other. In his analysis of multi-dimensional sociology, he provides an integrative model to understand the sociological approach.

Although his attempt to integrate macro-micro and relate action and order seems promising, Alexander adopts a minimal position. The problems in theorizing macro-micro are specific in one and the other. He rejects all theories (such as symbolic interactionism) that begin at the micro level with voluntary agency and build toward the macro level. From his point of view, these theories cannot deal with the *suigeneris* (society in itself) character of collective phenomena. He also rejects theories (such as exchange theory) that begin with rational action and link it to material

	ORDER COLLECTIVE	
	Material Structures	Norms
Action	Instrumental	Normative
	(Materialist)	(Idealist)
	Rational Action	Voluntary Agency

Figure 5.1: Alexander's Integrative Model
(Ritzer, 1988: 491)

structures like the economy (ibid.). Finally, Alexander rejects 'collectivist, rationalist', materialist theories (such as economic and structural determinism) that emphasize coercive order and eliminate individual freedom (ibid.). However, he tries to put collective order and individual freedom together. As he puts it, 'the hope for combining collective order and individual voluntarism lies within the normative rather than the rationalist tradition' (Alexander, 1982: 108).

However, Alexander suggests that social theorists must choose either a collectivist or an individualist perspective while taking precautions. For instance, 'if they choose a collectivist theory, they can incorporate a 'relatively small' element of individual negotiation. If, however, they choose an individual theory, they are doomed to the 'individual dilemma' of trying to sneak into their theory supra-individual phenomena to deal with the randomness inherent in their theory' (Ritzer, 1988: 492). This dilemma can only be resolved 'if the formal adherence to individualism is abandoned' (Alexander, 1982: 27).

Despite several promising features, Alexander ends his multi-dimensional sociology by emphasizing macro (subjective) phenomena. As a result, his contribution to developing a theory of macro-micro integration is considered relatively limited. However, his sociological approach seems quite exciting and provides a specific way to think about it.

KEY TERMS

Civil solidarity: It revolves around a distinctive type of universalizing community, an inclusive 'weness' that gradually comes to be defined and enforced. Alexander has discussed civil solidarity to describe civil society.

Cultural sociology: Cultural sociology is a principal focus of Alexander's current work. He characterized culture as a partially autonomous dimension of social life.

Functionalism: Functionalism views society as a system in which each part is related to the whole. Thus, society is patterned by monocausal factors of function.

Macro-micro theorizing: Alexander has attempted to bridge the gap between macro and micro theorizing. Micro perspective discusses norms and conditions, while macro emphasizes Parsons's tripartite model of culture, society and personality.

Multiculturalism: Alexander reconceptualizes multiculturalism as a discursive project, aiming at redefining the term of inclusion and characterizing it as a form of incorporation decidedly superior, sociologically and morally, to assimilation and 'hyphenation'.

Multidimensionality: It is the best known expression of Alexander's synthesizing ambition. Multidimensionality is a presuppositional synthesis aimed at breaking through this analytic impasse.

Neo-functionalism: Neo-functionalism is a self-critical strand of a functional theory that seeks to broaden functionalism's intellectual scope while retaining its theoretical core (https://www.yourarticlelibrary.com/essay/sociology-essay/neo-functionalism-a-discovery-and-reconstruction-of-functional-sociology/39917).

REFERENCES

Alexander, Jeffery, 'The "Individualist Dilemma" in Phenomenology and Interactionism', in S.N. Eisentadt and, in H.J. Helle (eds.), *Macro-Sociological Theory*, vol. 1, London: Sage Publications, 1985.

——, *Theoretical Logic in Sociology*, vol. 1, *Positivism, Presuppositions and Current Controversies*, Berkeley: Berkeley University, 1982.

Alexander, Jeffrey and Paul Colomy, 'Toward Neo-functionalism', *Sociological Theory*, 3, 1985.

Orru, Marco, *Review of Talcott Parsons: On Economy and Society* (by Robert J. Holten and Bryan S. Turner) and *The Integration of Economic and Sociological Theory* (The Marshall Lectures, University of Cambridge, 1953). *Contemporary Sociology 17*: 115-117.

Ritzer, George, *Sociological Theory*, Singapore: McGraw Hill Publishing Company, 1988.

CHAPTER 6

Neo-Marxism

After 1960, the classical sociological theory was subjected to several criticisms. During the 1980s, many sociological theories emerged, such as neo-functionalism, neo-Marxism, post-modernism and post-structuralism. However, with the disintegration of former Soviet Russia in August 1990, it lost the relevance of Marxism and the Marxian interpretation of capitalism. At this juncture, Fukuyama announced that it was the end of history. At this critical time, several Marxist theorists and thinkers came out to save the comprehensive nature of Marx's theory and established a new approach to sociology termed neo-Marxism. However, these theorists tried to maintain the originality of Marx's thoughts and claimed to work within the periphery of Marx's original work.

Some of the central issues associated with neo-Marxism are:

(*i*) The neo-Marxist theory is the extension of Marxism developed in the light of contemporary capitalism.
(*ii*) The significant sources of neo-Marxism are the writings of both Marx and Engels. Therefore, the central perspective of neo-Marxism is Marxism.
(*iii*) Neo-Marxism is based on Marx's conceptual, theoretical and methodological orientation.
(*iv*) The Marxian notion of 'working-class revolution' made ground for the development of neo-Marxism. It is because of Marx's prediction that the working-class revolution would not occur within the capitalist system.

Neo-Marxism has not established itself as a distinct sociological theory. It is loosely applied to any social theory or sociological analysis which draws on the ideas of Karl Marx and Friedrich Engels

(Neo-Marxist Theories: Useful Notes on Neo-Marxist Theories). This section will mainly focus on the neo-Marxian analysis of Habermas and Althusser.

I. JÜRGEN HABERMAS (1929-)

Jürgen Habermas belongs to the second generation of intellectuals of the Frankfurt School. Habermas was born on 18 June 1929 in Dusseldorf and grew up in Gummersbach. He described the surroundings of his childhood years during the Nazi regime as bourgeois, conformist and unpolitical. In his youth and study days, he experienced the shocking disclosures of the Nuremberg trials and the gradual post-war reconstruction of democracy. In 1961, he obtained a doctoral degree at the University of Marburg. He was one of the strong supporters of Marxism.

In the mid-sixties, Habermas became known as one of the young generations of proponents of so-called critical theory. Today, he is one of the most far-reaching and discussed philosophers and social theorists of the twentieth century. Habermas introduced his ideas energetically into the public political debate and provided intellectual resources for the student movement. Habermas reconstructed a wide variety of theories. He wanted to develop a rational reconstruction of studies and theories within sociology, psychology and philosophy to uncover any potential developments in social institutions, culture, language and personalities that might offer for extending the rational, argumentative dialogue and communication in modern society.

HABERMAS'S ANALYSIS OF 'THE PUBLIC SPHERE'

Habermas recognizes that many of Marx's ideas are still relevant. Marx identified many problems that existed in capitalist society. One of these problems is its tendency to produce economic depression or crisis. Here, it was needed to re-establish control over the financial process, which has come to control us more than we control (Giddens, 2004: 676). Habermas proposes that one of the main ways of achieving such increased control is by a revival of what he calls the 'public sphere'. Habermas discussed the concept of a *public sphere* in his first significant publication, *Structural Transformation of the Public Sphere.* He addresses this theme historically by examining the creation and development of the public sphere for political opinion forming among citizens from the eighteenth century. Turner defines the public sphere as:

> a realm of social life where people can bring up matters of general interest; where they can discuss and debate these issues without recourse to custom, dogma and force; and where they can resolve differences of opinion by rational argument (Turner, 2002: 190).

In this sense, the public sphere provides a framework for democracy.

Despite the democratic nature of the public sphere, Habermas argues, parliaments and parties do not provide us with a sufficient basis for collective decision-making. Here, emphasis on the necessity to renew the public sphere through the reform of democratic procedures and the more consistent involvement of community agencies and other local groups. At this point, modern means of communication could play a significant role in forming the public sphere. For example, clubs, cafes, journals, newspapers, public television, radio the internet offer many provide open dialogue and discussion. In the present time, the public sphere has become an acclamation forum for the administrators of power rather than a platform for open, mutual reasoning and opinion-forming. However, Habermas is fully aware of the severe hindrances that have always existed to accessing participatory opinion-forming, which are primarily conditioned by economics, class and gender.

THE THEORY OF COMMUNICATIVE ACTION

The theory of communicative action is one of the essential theories of sociology. Habermas discussed it in his two-volume book *The Theory of Communicative Action* (Habermas, 1984). He tries to build his theory based on several theoretical ideas. In Thomas

McCarthy's words, Habermas develops his ideas through: 'a somewhat unusual combination of theoretical constructions with historical reconstructions of the ideas of "classical" social theorists' (MacCarthy, in Habermas, 1984: vii).

In this sense, he did an exercise toward critiquing and utilizing the ideas of various social theorists, such as Marx, Weber, Durkheim, Mead, Lukacs, Horkheimer, Adorno and Parsons. Based on these exercises, Habermas summarized his theory as follows:

> If we assume that the human species maintains itself through the socially coordinated activities of its members and that this coordination is established through communication—and in certain spheres of life, through communication aimed at reaching agreement—then the reproduction of the species also requires satisfying the conditions of rationality inherent in communicative action (Habermas, 1984: 397).

Habermas provides greater analysis of this theory by combining both volumes. The first volume of *The Theory of Communicative Action* focuses on action and rationality. In the second volume, he introduces the concept of a system. He tries to connect it to micro-processes of action and interaction through a reconceptualization of the phenomenological concept of lifework. In a sense, volume 1 is Habermas's micro-sociology, whereas volume 2 is his macro-sociology.

From both volumes of *The Theory of Communicative Action*, Habermas summarized four types of action: (1) teleological, (2) normatively-regulated, (3) dramaturgical, and (4) communicative (Habermas cites in Turner, 2002: 203).

1. *Teleological action:* It is behaviour oriented to calculating various means and selecting the most appropriate means to realize explicit goals. Such action becomes strategic when other acting agents are involved in one's calculations. Habermas also calls this action 'instrumental' because it concerns the means to achieve ends. Most importantly, he emphasizes that this kind of action is too often considered 'rational action' in previous conceptualizations of rationality. For as he is to argue, this view of rationality is too narrow. It forces critical theory into a conceptual trap: if teleological or means-ends rationality is what

has taken over the modern world and what has, as a consequence, oppressed people, then how does critical theory propose rational alternatives? Wouldn't such a rational theory simply represent another oppressive application of means-ends rationality? The answer to these questions lies in recognizing that there are several types of action and that true rationality does not reside in teleological action but in communicative action.

2. *Normatively-regulated action:* It is behaviour oriented to a group's shared values. Thus, normative action is directed toward complying with normative expectations of collectively organized groupings of individuals.
3. *Dramaturgical action:* It is an action that involves conscious manipulation of oneself before an audience or public. It is ego-centred because it involves actors manipulating their behaviours to present their intentions. Still, it is also social in that such manipulation is done in the context of organized activity.
4. *Communicative action:* It is an interaction among agents who use speech and non-verbal symbols to understand their mutual situation and plans of action, or they can agree on how to coordinate their behaviours.

These four action types concern different kinds of 'worlds'. Turner (2002: 204) divided it into the (1) 'objective or external world' of manipulative objects, (2) the 'social world' of norms, values and other socially recognized expectations, and (3) the 'subjective world' of experiences. Teleological action is concerned primarily with the objective world, normatively regulated action with the social and dramaturgical action with the subjective and external. But it is only with communicative action that actors 'refers simultaneously to things in the objective, social and subjective worlds to negotiate common definitions of the situation' (Habermas, 1984: 95).

In this sense, Habermas is most interested in *communicative action*, or where:

the actions of the agents involved are coordinated not through egocentric calculations of success but through acts of *reaching an understanding.* In communicative action, participants are not primarily oriented to their own successes; they pursue their individual goals under the condition that they can *harmonize* their plans of action based on *common situation definitions* (ibid.).

Communicative action is potentially more rational than all the others because it deals with all three worlds. These worlds of communicative action clearly emphasize the importance of speech in communicative action. However, such action is broader than 'speech acts or equivalent non-verbal expressions' (ibid.: 278). In dealing with speech, Habermas argues that actors must know more than the linguistic rules of constructing sentences and talking; they must also master 'dialogue-constitutive universals', which are part of the 'social, linguistic structure of society'. At this point, Habermas proposes an ideal type of speech situation: 'in which actors possess all of the relevant background knowledge and linguistic skills to communicate without distortion' (Turner, 2002: 197).

In other words, Habermas is more interested in critically analysing distorted communication. Habermas tried to establish a society free from distorted communication. Marx's idea is relevant here, seeking to eliminate (capitalist) barriers to undistorted work and Habermas is interested in removing barriers to accessible communication. In other words, Marx was led to focus on work, whereas Habermas concentrated on communication. For Habermas, elements of undistorted communication are found in contemporary communication.

This brings us to the central issue of rationalization in Habermas's work. Habermas is influenced here not only by Marx's work but also by Weber's. The rationalization of communicative action leads to communication that is free from domination and is free and open. Rationalization involves emancipation, *removing restrictions on communication* (Habermas, 1970: 118). *Rationality* means the removal of the barriers that distort communication, but generally, it means a communication system in which ideas are openly presented and defended against criticism; unconstrained agreement develops during argumentation. To understand this better, we must distinguish between the previously discussed communicative action and discourse discussed by Habermas.

Communicative action occurs in everyday life, whereas the discourse is:

> That form of communication that is removed from contents of experience and action and whose structure assures us that the bracketed validity claims of assertions, recommendations, or warnings are the exclusive object of discussion; that participants, themes and contributions are not restricted except with reference to the goal of testing the validity claims in questions; that no force except that of the better argument is exercised; and that all motives except that of the cooperative search for truth are excluded (Habermas, 1975: 107-8).

Therefore, discourse is the 'ideal speech situation' in which force or power does not determine valid arguments. Instead, the weight of evidence and argumentation determines what is reasonable. The arguments that emerge from such a discourse are free and Habermas adopts a consensus theory of truth. This truth is part of all communication. As Thomas McCarthy says,

> The idea of truth points ultimately to a form of interaction that is free from all distorting influences. The good and true life 'that is the goal of critical theory is inherent in the notion of truth: it is anticipated in every act of speech' (MacCarthy cites in Ritzer, 1988: 258).

Thus, in the communicative action, actors interact, argue, use and simultaneously produce standard definitions of the situation. Such definitions are part of the lifeworld of society. If they have been produced and reproduced through communicative action, they are the basis for a society's rational and non-oppressive integration. For Habermas, the lifeworld is a 'culturally transmitted and linguistically organized stock of interpretative patterns'. The lifeworld is the world viewed from a participant's perspective and it is structured by meaningful symbols communicated through verbal action that is oriented toward understanding. This coordination and integration of action build on consensus established communicatively through recognizing the validity of verbal statements. In this context, Turner points out,

> Three components of the lifeworld culture, society, personality—meet corresponding needs of society cultural reproduction, social integration

and personality formation—through three dimensions along which communicative action is conducted reaching an understanding, coordinating interaction and socialization (Turner, 2002: 206).

As Habermas summarizes in volume 2:

In coming to an understanding with one another about their situation, participants in communication stand in a cultural tradition which they use and at the same time renew; in coordinating their actions via intersubjective recognition of criticizable validity claims, they rely upon their membership in groupings and at the same time reinforce their integration; through participating in the interaction with competent persons, growing children internalize capacities for action (Habermas, 1984: 208).

These lifeworld processes are interrelated with the system in a society. Action in economic, political, familial and other institutional contexts draws upon and reproduces the lifeworld's cultural, societal and personality dimensions.

In short, Habermas's theory of communicative action traces the conflict between, on the one hand, the rationalization of worldviews and early modernity on the other. The public sphere plays a more significant role in communicative action. It covers broader areas and underpins a communication theory of morality, law and democracy. This theory involves creating a rational space for communicative action.

HABERMAS ON NEO-MARXISM

Jürgen Habermas has been working on a detailed re-examination and synthesis of social thought in the light of the Frankfurt school of critical theory in general and Marxian theory in particular since the 1960s. The central question before neo-Marxism, as discussed by Habermas, is:

1. How is social theory to develop ideas that keep Karl Marx's emancipatory project alive?
2. How is social theory to confront Max Weber's historical analysis of rationalization in a way that avoids his pessimism and thereby keep Marx's emancipatory goals at the centre of theory?

3. How is social theory to avoid the retreat into subjectivism of earlier theorists such as Lukacs, Horkheimer and Adorno, who mainly focused on states of subjective consciousness within individuals and as a result, lost Marx's insight that society is constructed and sustain social relations among individuals?
4. How is social theory conceptualizing and developing a theory that reconciles the forces of material production and political organization? (Turner, 2002: 189).

Habermas has attempted to answer these questions in his neo-Marxist approach. However, Habermas's theories are essentially a composite of ideas drawn from various sources, such as social theory, linguistics, philosophy, and psychology. Habermas's view on neo-Marxism can be outlined in the following points:

1. Habermas wants to follow Marx in giving an account of the history of society as a process of development, in which things get better in the sense that societies become more complex and better adapted.
2. For Habermas, capitalism is more effective in organizing economic production than its predecessors.
3. Marx puts the growth of economic production at the centre of his conception of social development. In contrast, Habermas has moved it from this crucial position, seeing the growth of society's adaptability as a matter of learning and, thus, of the accumulation of knowledge.
4. Habermas argues that the pessimism of the Frankfurt school results from their limited conception of how knowledge is connected with human interests. Following Marx, theorists of the Frankfurt school have seen two main kinds of interest: *instrumental* and *emancipatory* interest. The instrumental and emancipatory interests are explained as Instrumental interest is concerned with the domination of nature to satisfy material needs. This interest also involves the domination of people to organize them into the required economic activity. The emancipatory interest is the desire to be freed of all oppression expressed in critical thinking. The Frankfurt school thought

that the emancipatory interest was effectively neutralized by the triumph of instrumental reason (Cuff et al., 1990: 126).

In addition to two types of interest, there is a third interest; the interest human beings have in understanding one another and in intelligibly communicating with one another. Habermas argues that this interest has not been effectively recognized at the centre of his analysis.

5. Habermas shifted from Marxian economic production of social organization to 'communication'. In addition, he has hope for a more significant role for rationality (i.e., reason) in society.
6. Habermas gives communication the central place by constructing rationality and truth as communication phenomena. He argues that truth is a matter of agreement. We arrive at the truth through discussion and argument amongst ourselves.
7. Unlike Marxists, Habermas does not propose that the working class is the force to produce social change. Indeed, the Marxists challenge him to nominate which groups in society will provide the energy necessary to transform society in these emancipatory ways.

However, in the course of communicative action, he accepts the decline of the sphere of 'public life' in capitalist society. In this sense, Habermas discusses the 'systematically distorted' communication in capitalist society. At this point, discourse does not proceed without interference and control and people are by no means counted as equal participants in debate in a society permeated by inequalities. In a capitalist society, Habermas argues, communication has built into it a discrepancy between those conditions required for the entire exercise of reason and the reaching of truth and those which govern how we talk to one another.

The intervention of the state and administrative regulation is increasing in more and more areas of social life. At this juncture, the legitimacy of the *status quo* based on the traditional structure would be disturbed and even destroyed. As a result, there are possibilities for a 'legitimacy crisis' that generates inequality in the advanced capitalist society. Further, there may also be 'rationality crises', resulting from the fact that the state, required to regulate the economy to sustain economic growth, will intervene more and more extensively in economic and social organization, becoming overburdened and incapable of satisfying all the different demands people make on it. Consequently, there will be dissatisfaction because the state does not provide what people want. In short, the state may be extending control in some ways, but simultaneously, it is creating questions about its legitimacy.

II. LOUIS ALTHUSSER (1918-1990)

Louis Althusser (1918-90) was the founder of Marxian structuralism. During the 1960s, there came a reaction against this tendency in thinking about Marx with Louis Althusser, the French theoretician, playing the central role. In this sense, he is also known for Marxist philosophy and conflict theory. He condemned theorists like Lukacs, Gramsci and the Frankfurt school for 'humanism'.

Althusser was born in Algeria in 1918 and moved to France with his parents in 1930. According to his biography, his childhood was miserable, characterized by an inner torment that perhaps accounts for his later recurrent depressions and final madness and personal tragedy. He was born and brought up as a catholic and spent much of the war in a German prisoner-of-war camp. After the close of the war, he came to École Normale Supérieure in Paris as a student and joined the French Communist Party. However, from the start, he was an independent-minded intellectual and came into repeated conflict with the party leadership, from whom he was increasingly estranged.

For Marx, a collection of essays is considered his best work, it appeared in France in 1965. Althusser influenced left social theory with his attempts to establish the theoretical interpretation of Marxism in terms that could be considered scientific. In many ways, Althusser's position among Marxists was comparable to that of Parsons among younger sociologists. For a while, his structuralism was the theory against which every serious Marxist was required to take a stand. His productive life ended tragically when he lost his sanity, strangled his wife to death and was committed to a mental institution in France.

ALTHUSSER ON NEO-MARXISM

The work of Louis Althusser is primarily defined by the nature of his focus on Marx's work. He wanted to deal with Marx's work properly. Althusser's work is best examined in the context of the debate surrounding Marx's work. Althusser's main focus begins with distinguishing between the 'young' Marx and the 'mature' Marx. 'Young' Marx is known for left-Hegelian humanist and historicist understanding and discusses the theory of alienation.

On the other hand, 'mature' or 'old' Marx involves discovering the operations of capitalist society that was both structured and scientific. The theory of alienation has been discussed in Marx's work *The Economic and Philosophic Manuscript,* which describes capitalist society in the *Capital.* To Althusser, '*The 1844 manuscript* was a concern for the devastating effect of the alienating conditions of capitalism on the individual' (Ritzer, 1988: 264).

In this sense, Althusser does not regard the young Marx as 'Marxist' and scientific. 'Youth Marx led to Marxism, but only at the price of a prodigious break with his origins, a heroic struggle against the illusions he had inherited from the Germany in which he was born and an acute attention to the realities concealed by these illusions' (Marx, 1970: 21).

Marx's early work's philosophical, humanistic and historical bases led him to centre on an active, creative and free actor.

On the contrary, Althusser believed that the heart of Marxist theory lies in the structure of society and the laws that govern the operation of these structures rather than with free actors. In his view, this focus emerges most clearly in the *Capital.* As Althusser said, 'If we take seriously what Marx tells us about the real dialectic of history, it is not 'men' who make history, although its dialectic is realized in them and their practice, but the masses in the relations of class struggle' (Althusser, 1977: 168).

There is, Althusser says, a decisive break between the early (young Marx) and later (mature Marx) works. This breaks what he calls an 'epistemological break' in the history of Marx's work and that Marx shifted from philosophical to abstract theory (Benton, 1984: 53). It is the shift from an ideological to a scientific position. After 1845, he moved toward a more scientific orientation. Althusser argued that in 1845, Marx made: 'a scientific discovery without historical precedent, in its nature and effects . . . Marx established a new *Science*: the science of the history of "social formation"' (Althusser, 1969: 13).

In other words, in the *Capital,* Marx developed a science, which is a science of social formation, *the socio-economic whole.* It is not a science of 'the subject'. 'The subject', which Lukacs, Gramsci and they have put at the centre of their attention, is an ideological creation. According to Althusser, the purpose of Marx's later theory is to expose the ideological nature of the concept of 'subject', not to put it at the centre of his science.

Ritzer here summarized his 'epistemological break' by outlining three significant points:

> (1) Marx developed a whole new set of concepts, replacing ideas like alienation, species-being and other humanistic concepts with a new set of scientific structural concepts such as social formations, superstructure, relations of production and forces of production; (2) Marx engaged in a theoretical critique of all varieties of philosophical humanism; and (3) Marx defined humanism as a form of ideology—an elitist and distorted idea system (Ritzer, 1988: 264-5).

Althusser concluded: 'This rupture with every *philosophical*. . . humanism is no secondary details; it is Marx's scientific discovery' (Althusser, 1969: 227).

In the neo-Marxian analysis, Althusser examined three significant components of social formation by rejecting the simple dichotomization of Marx's base structure and superstructure. The essential elements of a social formation are the economy, polity and ideology. The interaction of these structural components makes up the social whole at any given time.

Althusser's account of Marx is meant to retain the 'base/superstructures' idea, which he treats as a useful metaphor. Engels has explicitly made a point, acknowledging that only 'in the last analysis' does the economic base exercise a determining influence on other features of society. Althusser intends to retain this idea and speaks of the economic structure as a determinant in the last instance. In this sense, the economic structure is no longer seen as a straightforward determinant of the organization of society. It is because all social organizationss no longer have to be examined simply concerning the economic organization and activities. Althusser suggests another part of the social structure may be dominant. He draws a 'distinction between that structure (the economy) which is *determinant* (in the last instance) of features of the organization of the socio-economic whole and that structure which is, in any given historical context, the one which dominates the society, which he calls, 'the structure-in-dominance' (Cuff et al., 1990: 123).

The 'structure-in-dominance' can help understand the nature of various society types. In modern capitalism, the political sector dominates the economy and the state controls and intervenes in economic activity. In medieval society, by contrast, religion had a dominant position *vis-à-vis* both financial and political organizations. Thus, the structure 'in dominance' varies from society to society and from time to time. Still, the role of the economy as a 'determinant in the last instance' is preserved since the form of economic activity determines the possibilities for which particular other structures can be dominant. For example, the advanced state of capitalist economic organization allows the state to assume its dominant role.

Another fundamental element of social formation is the polity in which the state's role is essential. The state's role, Althusser goes on, is to secure the reproduction of the conditions of capitalist production, to endure those circumstances in which there will be no disruption of capitalist activity. Here, Althusser has discussed 'the ideological state apparatus'. This apparatus includes various institutions, such as religious and educational organizations, trade unions, political parties, the media and culture (ibid.: 123-4). For Althusser, these institutions are counted as part of the *state* apparatus rather than as private.

The third essential element of social formation is ideology, as discussed by Althusser. Althusser's argument on ideology differs from that of Marx. It is thought that ideology consists of false ideas made necessary by society's class-divided, exploitative nature so that ideology would disappear with the abolition of societies organized in this way culture (ibid.: 124). Althusser does not think that this will occur. Althusser here made a distinction between ideology and science. Ideology, he wrote, 'is distinguished from science in that the practico-social function is more important than the theoretical function (function as knowledge)' (Althusser, 1969: 231).

At this point in Althusser's thinking, ideology is 'the lived relation between men and their world' (ibid.: 233). This relation is both real, in the sense that it describes real historical social relations and how people are positioned in them and imaginary, in the sense that it is in ideology that conservative or revolutionary *will* is expressed. As a general system of representations, ideology for Althusser was an 'organic' or 'indispensable' part of the social totality and he maintained thought ideology would always be present even in a future society.

Althusser criticized economic determinists for defining economic factors as always occupying the principal position and other factors, such as politics and ideology, as always occupying the role of a secondary factor. In Althusser's view, social institutions other than the economy can occupy a position of pre-eminence, at least for a time. For instance, the educational sector plays the dominant ideological role. This sector essentially prepares the young for a compliant role in productive activity, equipping them with the knowledge to do the relevant work and with attitudes, making them accept authority. Althusser has made a significant attempt to discover the hidden ideas of Marx and the relevance of various structural forms of society in social formation.

KEY TERMS

Communicative action: Action-oriented toward understanding, that is, action based on a consensus of definitions regarding situations dependent upon the mutual recognition of perceptions of the environment, social norms and the identities of individuals.

Discourse ethics: A theory of morality claiming that moral norms concerning justice can be tested rationally in an argumentative dialogue.

Dramaturgical action: It is an action that involves conscious manipulation of oneself before an audience or public.

Formal pragmatics: A theory of rational communication oriented toward understanding. Habermas applies a sensible reconstruction of these principles to demonstrate that rational communication can include three validity questions: truth, rightness and truthfulness.

Ideology: According to Althusser, ideology is the *lived* relation between men and their world.

Knowledge-constitutive interests: These express the perspectives and cognitive strategies on which human beings base their cognition of reality; knowledge is tied to fundamental interests in the history of the human species: the technical, the practical and the emancipatory.

Lifeworld: A stock of meaning patterns constituting the basis for communicative action. Lifeworld is reproduced and organized linguistically. It can be perceived as the worldview from the participant's perspective comprising culture, the social world and personality.

Normative action: Behaviour oriented to a group's shared values. Habermas discussed it in his analysis of the theory of communicative action.

Public sphere: The public sphere is a realm of social life where people can bring up matters of general interest, where they can discuss and debate these issues without recourse to custom, dogma and force, and where they can resolve differences of opinion by rational argument.

Strategic action: Social action is based on selfish, purposive, rational calculations to determine which actions best fulfil the goals stipulated as a priority. The analyses include the influence of decisions taken by the actors.

System: Social systems on which purposive rational action is organized and coordinated through the institutionalized steering media of money and power. The system functions independently of mutual understanding and communication on situational definitions and social norms.

Teleological action: Behaviour oriented to calculating various means and selecting the most appropriate means to realize explicit goals.

REFERENCES

Althusser, Louis, *For Marx,* Harmondsworth: Penguin, 1969.

——, *Politics and History*, London: NLB, 1977.

Benton, Ted, *The Rise and Fall of Structural Marxism: Althusser and His Influence*, New York: St. Martin's, 1984.

Cuff, E.C., W.W. Sharrock and D.W. Francis, *Perspectives in Sociology*, London: Unwin Hyman, 1990.

Giddens, Anthony, *Sociology*, 4th edition, Oxford: Polity, 2004.

Habermas, Jürgen, *Legitimation Crisis*, Boston: Beacon Press, 1975.

——, *The Theory of Communicative Action,* 2 vols., Boston: Beacon Press, 1984.

——, *The Theory of Communicative Action,* vol. 2, entitled *Lifeword and System: and Lifeworld A Critique of Functional Reason*, Boston: Beacon Press, 1984.

——, *Toward a Rational Society*, Boston: Beacon Press, 1970.

MacCarthy cites Ritzer, George, *Sociological Theory*, Singapore: McGraw-Hill Publishing Company, 1988.

MacCarthy, Thomas, 'Translator Introduction', in Habermas, Jürgen, *The Theory of Communicative Action,* 2 vols., Boston: Beacon Press, 1984.

Marx, Karl, Preface to the French edition, *Capital*, vol. 1, London: Lawrence and Wishart, 1970.

Ritzer, George, *Sociological Theory*, Singapore: McGraw-Hill Publishing House, 1988.

Turner, Jonathan H., *The Structure of Sociological Theory*, Jaipur: Rawat Publications, 2002.

CHAPTER 7

Post-Structuralism and Post-Modernism

Post-structuralism and post-modernism both have their roots in structuralism. Structuralism is considered a theoretical approach to linguistics and semiotics. However, it became influential in many disciplines, such as philosophy, social theory, linguistics, literacy criticism, cultural analysis, psychoanalysis, the history of ideas, the philosophy of science, anthropology, etc. The concept of 'structuralism' refers to understanding how the organization of the whole society shapes or structures individual behaviour. On the other, the different meaning is associated with the work of Claude Levi-Strauss, who sees individual behaviour shaped, albeit unconsciously, by underlying structures of language and meaning. The approach has come to be called *structuralism.*

Ferdinand de Saussure (1857-1913) made a critical move toward a different sense of structuralism with the distinction between *parole* (or speech) and *langue* (or the language system). He declared that *langue,* not parole, is the object of scientific linguistic study. Language is a system of signs. The key question is one of meaning. How do signs get their meaning? A standard answer is that signs get their meaning through what they stand for encouraging us to try to see how a given sign (word) means what it does by seeing how it relates to what it stands for. Saussure takes two steps away from this position:

(1) The sign gets its meaning from and within the system, so we seek to understand how it does by looking at its relation to the rest of the system. (2) The sign gets its meaning within the system from the ways it *contrasts* with other signs in the system (Cuff et al., 1990: 128).

The critical consideration in the language system is making the difference at the level of sound and the words.

POST-STRUCTURALISM

The origin of post-structuralism goes back to Ferdinand Saussure's structuralism, as discussed earlier. Structuralism has given the idea that a language creates its objects. Here, structuralism states that the meaning of a word depends upon its relationships with other words.

It is challenging to pinpoint when structuralism ended and post-structuralism began. However, Charles Lemert (1990) traces the beginning of post-structuralism to a 1966 speech by Jacques Derrida, one of the acknowledged leaders of this approach, in which he proclaimed the dawning of a new post-structuralist age from much of the philosophical background of post-modern theory. Indeed, nowadays, post-structuralism is often seen as a post-modern philosophy. George Ritzer has defined post-structuralism in the following words:

> Post-structuralism has come as a reaction to structuralism. We can define post-structuralism as a rebellion against structuralism. We can define post-structuralism as a school of thought that builds upon but seeks to distance itself from the structuralism associated with thinkers like Ferdinand Saussure, Ronald Barthes, Claude Lévi-Strauss, Louis Althusser, etc.

Post-structuralism, therefore, emerged as a theoretical approach in reaction to structuralism. This approach was re-established by considering the problems and difficulties associated with structuralism. The following characteristics of post-structuralism can be outlined as follows:

1. The birth of post-structuralism lies in the corrected version of traditional structuralism. The philosophical background of post-modern theory influences it.
2. Structuralism emphasizes on subjectivity, whereas post-structuralism is concerned with objectivity.
3. Post-structuralism is eclectic because it includes structuralism and other theoretical perspectives.

4. Traditional structuralism is associated with the modern world, whereas post-structuralism is with the post-modern society.
5. In post-structuralism, there will not be any negligence of weaker sections of society. This period will be devoted to the welfare of depressed sections of society.
6. Post-structuralism involves society's diversity rather than unity. Post-structuralists tend to disrupt the notion of stability or unity of meaning.
7. Structuralists claimed that in a language, no sign had a positive meaning on its terms. Meaning is always a product of difference. Despite this, the structuralists considered language a relatively fixed, stable and even tyrannical structure.
8. In structuralism, a text is often seen as complete. Post-structuralism is always unfinished, full of holes and contradictory.

Despite many characteristics, as outlined above, post-structuralism always emphasizes that language produces meaning and does not express individuality. In short, post-structuralism is an approach or method that explores the relationships between language and knowledge and between knowledge and power meaningfully.

POST-MODERNISM

The advocates of post-modernity claim that the classical social thinkers took their inspiration from the idea that history has a shape and leads to progress, but now this notion has collapsed. There are no longer any 'grand narratives' or 'metanarratives' that make any sense. Baudrillard, Lyotard and Lacan argue that post-modernism is a historical stage in which narratives have lost meaning and applicability. It is because all that can be experienced has already been experienced. Therefore, the post-modern is a post-history epoch when nothing new can be said or felt. In this sense, this period is dominated by the new media, which 'take us out' of our past. Post-modern society is highly pluralistic and diverse. Despite having little content of the geographical area, we have come into contact with many ideas and values through the media and internet facilities worldwide. One of the critical post-modernist theorists is the French author Jean Baudrillard, who believes that the electronic media have destroyed our relationship to our past and created a chaotic, empty world.

Post-modernist theorists have also taken the idea from Saussure's structuralism. Baudrillard explains Saussure's idea that meanings are created by making connections between words instead of external reality. Here, Baudrillard clarifies more precisely that in a media-dominated age, meaning is produced by the flow of images in visual media. In this sense, media images make us closer to each other than any actual personal contact. We can watch everything on TV or the internet that is happening in the world. Baudrillard rightly speaks of 'the dissolution of life into TV'. The various views of post-modernity can be outlined in the following points:

(*i*) Post-modernity is a pluralization of lifeworlds—Zygmunt Bauman.
(*ii*) Post-modernity is the antithesis of class society—Pakulski and S. Crook.
(*iii*) Post-modernity is fragmentation, conflict and discontinuity—Jacques Derrida.
(*iv*) Post-modernity is based on the power-knowledge relationship—Michel Foucault.

However, the various viewpoints about post-modernism could not touch upon the characteristics of post-modernity; it needs to extend to the following:

1. Post-modernity rejects the limitation of all the subjects and suggests a need to construct a synthetic perspective to understand traditional structuralism, Marxism, and Feminism in a precise manner.
2. Post-modernists reject grand narratives and theories and establish an approach based on a micro-level that will make us understand the problem related to a particular place in a specific time.
3. Lyotard has opposed Marxism and Functionalism. At the same time, he rejects the great stories of tradition but emphasizes the little stories of that particular place.

4. Post-modernism emphasizes language because it is used as a medium of communication that spreads our ideas in various places. However, they accept the importance of computers and media in the post-modern world. In a broader sense, these communication mediums are involved in developing our knowledge. In other words, it is becoming an information-based society that makes us more intelligent; as a result, society will become more powerful.
5. Post-modernist theorists also reject the importance of modern art. Lyotard discussed three types of art—religious, court and bourgeoisie art. He left all forms of art.
6. Post-modernism relates to the cultural realm in which it is argued that post-modern products have tended to supplant modern products.
7. The major thrust of post-modernism is that everything in this society is superficial and provisional.
8. The world of society is entirely fragmented into varying cultures, ethnicities and pluralities based on differences in the way of life and attitude. The difference is the key variable that may help us understand this world.
9. Post-modern theorists argue that the necessity of human beings does not fulfil the present scientific knowledge because it needs to provide an understanding of skills and technology. Derrida follows it and says that knowledge is always limited by the institutions in which it is created. From this perspective, scientists can have no more direct access to the 'truth' than philosophers or historians.
10. Post-modernists argue that social sciences cannot comprehend society's reality or truth. Jean Baudrillard says simulacra, signs and symbols always construct it. Simulacra is the world of hyperreality, which does not have original copies of reality.
11. Post-modernity has been established on the belief that the modern era will end. In this sense, contemporary social theory sought a universal, ahistorical, rational foundation for analysing and critiquing society. At the same time, post-modern thinking rejects this 'foundationalism' and tends to be relativistic, irrational and nihilistic.

I. MICHEL FOUCAULT (1926-1984)

Paul-Michel Foucault (1926-84) was one of the most influential social theorists of the later part of the twentieth century. He was initially trained as a psychiatrist. He wrote many books, including *Birth of the Clinic* (1973) and *Madness and Civilization* (1965). Still, very soon, he turned against the medical profession by claiming that the body was a political object of power and that knowledge about it was always inseparable from power relations. Foucault was creative by nature and he maintained originality in thought. He was influenced by postwar French thinkers such as Dumezil, Canguilhem Bachelard, and Nietzsche Bataille and Freud was.

Foucault was born in Poitiers on 15 October 1926. When the war ended in 1945, he came to Paris and entered the Elite University, the École Normale Supérieure, in 1946, receiving his primary degree in philosophy and psychology. In 1961, he received the highest French Doctoral degree, with *Madness and Civilisation* as his dissertation. In 1962, he became a professor of philosophy at Clermont-Ferrand University and during the following years, he was a visiting professor in Tunis. During this time, he published *The Birth of the Clinic* [1973 (1963)] and *The Order of Things* [1970 (1966)]. In 1975, he published *Discipline and Punish* (English translation 1997), a study that marked a heightened interest in the disciplining effects of power. The power analysis is also at the Centre of his subsequent work, the first volume of *The History of Sexuality*, published in 1976 (English translation 1978). The second and third parts of this work were not published until 1984. The first volume of *The History of Sexuality* discusses the status of sexuality, mainly about the last two centuries. The other two volumes, *The Use of Pleasure* and *The Care of the Self* are about Greece and Rome. All these volumes on sexuality draw from his personal experience of sodomy. His formulation of knowledge and power also draws from power games of sodomy. Michel Foucault reportedly died in Paris on 25 June 1984, of AIDS.

Major sociological works:

1. *The Birth of the Clinic* (1963)
2. *Madness and Civilization* (1961)
3. *The Order of Things* (1966)
4. *The Archeology of Knowledge* (1969)
5. *Discipline and Punish* (1975)
6. *The History of Sexuality*, (2 vols.) (1976)
7. *Power and Knowledge: Selected Interviews and Other Writings* (1980)
8. *The Care of the Self* (1978)

FOUCAULT'S IDEA ON KNOWLEDGE AND POWER

Foucault, one of the two most prominent post-structuralists, came to talk of 'knowledge and power' to emphasize this intimate conjunction. Foucault adopts Nietzsche's interest in the relationship between power and knowledge, but that link is analysed more sociologically by Foucault. Foucault's analysis of knowledge and power is very much discussed in the social domain.

Foucault's main emphasis here is to enquire how knowledge domains have been formed based on social practices. These inquiries are conducted historically to prove that social practices engender domains of expertise that which bring to light new concepts and give rise to new subjects of expertise. Such an inquiry stands in clear opposition to Western philosophy, which assumes a stable source as the basis of human knowledge and academic Marxism, particularly assumes that human subjects and forms of knowledge are given beforehand the economic and social conditions of existence are imprinted on this given subject. On the other, Foucault deals with power relations in personal conduct and freedom politics. It raises the overwhelming issue of how power relations are a driving force in historical change.

Foucault maintains that at any given time in society, it is possible to investigate a dimension of knowledge that regulates the functioning of the people's thoughts. Foucault was dedicated to identifying the historical origins of the modern conception of the idea of the individual (particularly the individual mind). He, therefore, analysed the formation of the various 'discourses'. The discourses are the 'material manifestations of the thought that is preserved, transmitted and still affects our present-day thinking'. The nature of this discursive power attracts Foucault. His archaeological analysis 'individualizes and describes discursive formations'. Hence, he isolates ruptures, gaps, thresholds, breaks and discontinuities in any social formation and subjects them to close examination. To quote Foucault,

> The horizon of archaeology, therefore, is not a science, a rationality, a mentality, a culture; it is a tangle of interpositives whose limits and points of intersection cannot be fixed in a single operation. Archaeology is a comparative analysis that is not intended to reduce the diversity of discourses and to outline the unity that must totalize them but to divide their diversity into different figures. The archaeological comparison does not have a unifying but a diversifying effect.

More specifically, Foucault was interested in the basic discursive practices that formed the base of scientific discourse, particularly in the human sciences. However, the fact is that this view was silent on the issue of power and the link between knowledge and power.

Foucault later discusses the 'genealogy of power' (the natural successor to the archaeology of knowledge) in the Nietzschean sense to mean the analysis of the modalities of power. Knowledge and power ought to be distinguished from each other. Knowledge is a function of human interests and power relations. Genealogy is a method of understanding the mutual connections between systems of truth and modalities of power. Truth is always linked to power. Power can never be thought of in isolation; it is exercised through social practice and production. It is not applied externally through coercion or force but is circulated by practices that influence people to think, act and behave in a particular way. Hence, power constitutes a way of social cohesion and life. Foucault, therefore, reconceptualizes power and hegemony in a positive manner. He proves that it is part and parcel of our life without trying to legitimize power. It is indispensable to our existence. It operates in an impersonal way, not through an external agency. 'Power is exercised rather than possessed.' It is a strategy in which the dominating and dominated are jointly engaged. One conspires with the other in its exercise. Foucault breaks the traditional bond between power and repression and, in doing so, holds that to live socially is to be involved in power relations and that is only the truth above it. He maintains that beyond power, there is only more power.

In *The Genealogy of Power*, Foucault is concerned with how people govern themselves and others through knowledge production. 'Among other things, he sees knowledge generating power by constituting people as subjects and then governing the subjects with the knowledge' (Ritzer, 1988: 464).

Foucault is critical of the hierarchization of knowledge because it is based on the ranking systems of knowledge, which forms stratification in power. In this sense, he is more interested in seeing the structural relationships between knowledge and power.

His work *Discipline and Punish* (1975) shows the relationship between knowledge and power. In his work, Foucault is concerned about the period between 1757 and the 1830, during which prisoners' torture was replaced by prison rules' control over them (ibid.: 467). The general view is that this shift from torture to rules represented a humanization of the treatment of criminals in the form of more kind, less painful and less cruel. Thus, punishment, Foucault argues, became more rationalized. The new system of rules was 'more regular, more effective, more constant and more detailed in its effects; in short, which increase its effects while diminishing its economic cost' (Foucault, 1979: 80-81).

The link between knowledge and power was evident in the case of torture.

Another application of the relationship between knowledge and power can be seen in the first volume of *The History of Sexuality* (1980). To Foucault, sexuality is 'an especially dense transfer point for relations of power' (Foucault, 1980: 103). He sees his goal as being to 'define the regime of power-knowledge-pleasure that sustains the discourse on human sexuality in our part of the world' (ibid.: 11).

The History of Sexuality is a genealogical study of sex from the early Greek civilization onwards. Foucault here recognizes that power is 'productive'. Foucault suggests that talking about sex is not a sign of our freedom but rather a result of the fact that we are compelled to talk about it. Thus, power has 'produced' a vast discourse on sexuality and extended its hold over us even further, for, as indicated, going control requires access to our thoughts. If we do not talk about sex by keeping it private, we escape the reach of power. If we are compelled to talk about sex, we make it public and so amenable to surveillance and regulation. He, therefore, examines the way that sex is put into discourse and the way that power permeates that discourse.

Finally, Foucault has analysed the present history of human society. He was inconsistent in his thought; hence, it is difficult to examine the relationship between power and knowledge in general and its application in *Discipline and Punish* and *The History of Sexuality*. He also tried to find the truth produced only by multiple forms of constraint. More broadly, his contributions to social sciences are considered innovative in approach and practical methods.

II. JACQUES DERRIDA (1930-2004)

Jacques Derrida, a French thinker, was born near Algiers in 1930. Derrida is described as a linguistic philosopher rather than a sociologist. He has made a significant contribution to philosophy, linguistics and humanities. After the announcement of Charles Lemert, Derrida talked about the dawn of post-structuralism and post-modernism. Derrida was famous for his deconstruction theory, grammatology and writings. Derrida created a writing science called 'grammatology' as a post-modern thinker.

Major sociological works:

1. *Speech and Phenomena* (1973)
2. *Of Grammatology* (1976)
3. *Writing and Difference* (1978)
4. *Margins of Philosophy* (1981)
5. *Circumfession* (with Geoffrey Bennington) (1993)
6. *Specters of Marx* (1993)

DERRIDA ON DECONSTRUCTION

Derrida has developed a method or a theory of deconstruction. The primary aim of establishing a deconstruction method is to discover a text's hidden meaning. Here, Derrida was also against producing any concepts or theories because these concepts did not help us to know reality. According to Derrida, deconstruction will make us aware of the delusory nature of our attempts to come to a unified understanding of things. The literary meaning of deconstruction is a critical technique, especially in literary criticism, which claims that there is no single innate meaning and, thus, no correct interpretation of a text. Deconstruction involves finding out the meaning of meaning. In doing that, it deconstructs the explicit meaning of the text and tries to find out the hidden meaning, which is implicit. For example, the text *Mahabharata* gives meaning in that several meanings of fighting are related to it if injustice is done to us. Deconstruction is mainly related to his concept of text and writing. George Ritzer explains deconstruction below:

Deconstruction, as developed by Jacques Derrida, is a critical method that involves analysing a text to uncover its underlying contradictions and concealments. This process is ongoing and never definitive, as the goal is not to discover a fixed truth but to continually deconstruct and reveal the instability and complexity of the text. Through deconstruction, Derrida seeks to expose the power dyamics and tensions that shape the text, rather than to arrive at a definitive interpretation or understanding. This approach emphasizes the provisional and context-dependent nature of meaning (Ritzer, 1997).

It is challenging to define deconstruction in a precise term. However, post-modernists and Derrida, in particular, have tried to explain deconstruction by breaking the narratives into different textual elements and fragments. At this point, the word gains meaning as a part of a sentence.

The significant characteristics of deconstruction are:

1. Deconstruction is the theoretical approach and method of inquiry.
2. It tries to find out the hidden meaning of the text, i.e., it involves uncovering the meaning within the meaning.

3. It is against establishing any concepts and theories because it does not help us know the reality.
4. It is a critical technique.
5. Deconstruction involves breaking down the narratives into different textual elements and fragments and trying to understand hidden facts and their meaning.
6. Deconstruction is a post-structural blend of philosophy and linguistic and literary analysis.
7. Deconstruction is a critical technique used in the reading of texts. In this sense, the texts are open to criticism. We can arrive at truth only through the critical analysis of the text.
8. A text gives several meanings. It depends on the form of grammar and method of writing.
9. It gives contextual meaning to the reader rather than the author's intention of historical context or any of his particular contexts.
10. Derrida suggests to the reader and analyst that they must approach the text with the awareness of the arbitrariness of sign and meaning.

DERRIDA ON GRAMMATOLOGY AND WRITING

Derrida has created a science of writing that he calls 'grammatology.' Derrida, here, tries to locate the problems in the tradition of philosophy in the form of language. Derrida argues that philosophical tradition looked upon language as potentially a servant of thought and as an instrument in acquiring knowledge. Philosophers usually contrast the philosophical and literary. Literary writing is treated as a collection of misleading tricks and philosophers are therefore required to purge their writings of literary devices and effects. Derrida completely rejects this approach that philosophy itself is thoroughly literary.

The philosophical tradition has, therefore, been concerned with working out how the subject can master language. One, the structuralists have undermined it by showing that the language system produces meaning rather than the subject. Derrida goes one step forward and emphasizes that language creates meaning at the end of the line. He argues that: 'language always can produce meaning in ways that writers and speakers cannot control' (Cuff et al., 1990: 136).

Derrida here *deconstructed* language and reduced it to 'writing'. Derrida saw social institutions as nothing but writing and, therefore, unable to constrain people.

Contrary to the view of the structuralists that order and stability exist in the language system, Derrida sees language as disorderly and unstable. This is because different contexts give words different meanings. As a result, the language system cannot have constraining power over people. Furthermore, scientists can't search for the underlying laws of language. Thus, Derrida offers a subversive, deconstructive perspective that becomes important with the emergence of post-modernism and it is post-structuralism that laid the groundwork for post-modernism.

Derrida was hostile to the concept of 'logocentrism' that had dominated Western social thought. Logocentrism is the search for a universal system of thought that reveals what is true, correct, beautiful and so on. The approach of logocentrism involves, as Derrida describes, the 'historical repression and suppression of writing since Plato' (Derrida, 1978: 196). Logocentrism has led to the closure of philosophy and the human sciences. Derrida is interested in deconstructing or dismantling the source of this suppression—thereby writing from the things that enslave it. Derrida's deconstruction could be best described as 'the deconstruction of logocentrism' (ibid.: 230).

One of Derrida's writing aims is the attempt of literary criticism to look for a unified organization within writings, to look for a coherence of theme and design which coordinates all the aspects of work. Derrida's method highlights how literary texts defy this kind of treatment. He brings out the extent to which their organization could be more cohesive, with different aspects working against one another rather than contributing to some single theme. The critics' attempts to impose unity upon text can be considered deconstructive. By attempting to overcome this problem, the critics reproduce the difficulties they try to eliminate.

An excellent example of Derrida's thinking could be seen in his discussion of the 'theatre of the cruelty'. He contrasts this concept against the traditional theatre, which he sees as dominated by a system of thought that he calls 'representational logic'. Representational logic is a similar logic that has dominated social theory. In this sense, stage representation manifests 'real life'. It also fulfilled the expectations of writers, directors and so on. This 'representationalism' is the theatre's god, rendering the traditional theatre theological. A theological theatre is a controlled, enslaved theatre.

The stage is theological for as long as its structure, following the entire tradition, comports the following elements:

> An author-creator who, absent and from afar, is armed with a text and keeps watch over, assembles and regulates the time or the meaning of representation. . . . He lets representation represent him through representatives, directors or actors and *enslaved* interpreters . . . who . . . more or less directly represent the thought of the 'creator'. *Interpretive slaves* faithfully execute the providential designs of the 'master'. . . . Finally, the theological stage comports a passive, seated public, a public of spectators, consumers, of enjoyers (Derrida, 1978: 235).

Contrary to the traditional form of theatre, Derrida proposed an alternative stage in which 'speech will cease to govern the stage' (ibid.: 239). This stage will no longer be governed by authors and texts. Hence, actors will be free from the dictation of authors. Derrida has deconstructed the traditional theatre and suggests: 'the theatre of cruelty without economy, without reserve, without return, without history' (ibid.: 247).

In short, Derrida wants to see us free from the dictatorship of the writer and tries to establish a society that will be free from the ideas of all the intellectual authorities who have created the dominant discourse.

Having debunked Western logocentrism and the intellectual authority of writers, in the end, Derrida leaves us without an answer to how we carry forward in the process of writing, acting and so on. However, Derrida conveys much as a post-structuralist and postmodernist to understand present-day sociology and philosophy.

III. ANTHONY GIDDENS (1938-)

Anthony Giddens is considered one of Britain's modern social theorists. Like other social theorists, he has been wholly involved in the theoretical interpretation of human action and institutional processes in the social sciences and humanities. Giddens has drawn from an eclectic array of theoretical traditions in the social sciences, including hermeneutics, ethnomethodology, systems theory, psychoanalysis, structuralism and post-structuralism. Out of these diverse conceptual traditions, Giddens has developed a novel sociological approach that he terms 'structuration theory', a theoretical analysis of the relationship between self and society, emphasizing the processes of social reproduction and institutional transformation.

Giddens was born in London in 1938 and was educated at the University of Hull, where he got a BA degree with honours in Sociology. At the London School of Economics, he earned a Master's degree. He spent the better part of his academic career at the faculty of social and political sciences at the University of Cambridge. During this time, he wrote an extraordinary number of sociological tracts, including his best-selling textbook *Capitalism and Modern Social Theory* (1971), *The Class Structure of the Advanced Societies* (1973), *Central Problems in Social Theory* (1979), *A Contemporary Critique of Historical Materialism* (1981), *The Nation-State and Violence* (1986) and *Politics, Sociology and Social Theory* (1995). In fact, between 1971 and 1990, Anthony Giddens produced twenty-four books (sixteen of these single-authored, including four collections of his articles). Between 1989 and 1991, four significant commentaries on Giddens' work also appeared, reflecting the undoubted current 'star' status of Giddens as a social theorist.

Furthermore, his work can be divided into two periods. First, he developed his so-called structuration theory from the early 1970s until the mid-1980s. The main focus of the second period, from the mid-1980s until today, is the sociological analysis of modern society.

Major sociological works:

1. *Capitalism and Modern Social Theory* (1971)
2. *Politics and Sociology in the Thought of Max Weber* (1972)
3. *The Class Structure of the Advanced Societies* (1973)
4. *Positivism and Sociology* (ed.) (1974)
5. *New Rules of Sociological Method* (1976)
6. *Studies in Social and Political Theory* (1977)
7. *Émile Durkheim* (1978)
8. *Central Problems in Social Theory* (1979)
9. *A Contemporary Critique of Historical Materialism* (1981)
10. *Sociology: A Brief but Critical Introduction* (1982)
11. *Profiles and Critiques in Social Theory* (1983)
12. *The Constitution of Society* (1984)
13. *The Nation-State and Violence* (1986)
14. *Social Theory and Modern Sociology* (1987)
15. *The Consequences of Modernity* (1990)
16. *Modernity and Self-Identity* (1991)
17. *The Transformation of Intimacy* (1992)
18. *Beyond Left and Right: The Future of Radical Politics* (1994)
19. *In Defence of Sociology* (1996)
20. *Sociology*, 4th edition (2004)

ANTHONY GIDDENS'S STRUCTURATION THEORY

Anthony Giddens's structuration theory is one of the best-known and most articulated efforts to integrate agency and structure, micro and macro. Giddens (1976: 8) began 'introducing' this theory in the 1970s, but it appeared in his book *The Constitution of Society* (1984), which is subtitled *Outline of the Theory of Agency.* In his work, Giddens says, 'Every research investigation in the social sciences or history relates action to structure. There is no sense in which structure "determines" action or vice versa' (Giddens, 1984: 219).

Giddens' structuration theory combines diverse theories such as structural functionalism, action sociology, social interactionism,

Marxism, Weberian and Durkheimian. He wanted to create a foundation for a theory that would highlight the unique character of modern society. It takes a different and new sociological theory that transcends the foundational problems in classical sociology. However, he acknowledges that modern social sciences should reread classical sociologists to gather inspiration for a modern and more contemporary sociological theory (Giddens, 1971).

Giddens begins his discussion by dividing sociological theory into two groups—a group of theories that view society from a system or structure perspective and often unintentionally ignore the significance of the acting actor. Functionalism, structuralism and parts of Marxism belong to this group. The other group takes its point of departure in actors and their actions. The actors and the sum of their actions make up society and no structures or systems are independent of the actors. The strong emphasis on the individual and his actions in action sociological theories leads to a need for an adequate understanding of social institutions. As exponents of this approach, Giddens mentions theories of social interaction of Max Weber, George Herbert Mead, Erving Goffman, Harold Garfinkel, Alfred Schutz, rational choice theory and parts of Marxism, including analytical Marxism. Both two sociological theories create a conflict between agent and structure. In other words, the two sociological theories came up with very different answers to questions such as:

To what degree can we create our own lives and frames for our lives and to what degree are we already constrained by society and its structures when we are born? (*Structuration Theory: Meaning and Major Features*, retrieved on 25 January 2023).

Giddens describes this conflict between the individual and society as a dualism between an actor (the acting individual) and structure (society). He claims that this dualism must be transcended if sociology wants to comprehend more adequately the complexity of modern society. Structuration theory was developed to overcome this dualism. According to Giddens, structuration theory was developed as a result of critical dialogue with the major schools of social theory: sociological theories of action, functionalism, structuralism and Marxism.

In addition, Giddens also addresses the issue of macro-micro. Ritzer summarized it into two points:

> First, he feels that macro and micro are often pitted against one another by sociologists and he does not believe that one should have priority over the other. Second, even when there is a conflict between macro and micro, there is a tendency for a dysfunctional division of labour to develop among sociological theories. That is, theories like symbolic interactionism tend to focus on the activities of free actors. In contrast, theories like structural functionalism devote their attention to structural constraint.

Ultimately, Giddens concludes, 'the micro/macro distinction is not a particularly useful one'. The main thrust is that a rigid distinction between micro and macro is useless. In this sense, we need not use the macro-micro terminology, but we must deal with interrelationships, as Giddens proposes. Here, micro theoretical orientation seems more related to the actor and macro to the structure.

In the development of structuration theory, Giddens believes that it is a severe mistake that sociology mainly uses *either* actor or structure as its point of departure. Instead, he claims that the actor-structure relation fundamentally must be seen as a *duality of structure.* He means a coherent relation in which structure is the medium and outcome of the actor's action. For example, when I get on a bus, I produce and reproduce a structure, the public bus system, which is connected with many rules and routines: I have to buy a ticket, know when the bus leaves, refrain from smoking on the bus, etc. When I take the bus, I use existing structures and simultaneously, I create these structures the minute I step on the bus. This way, society is constantly made in a continuous structural process. Giddens calls this process social practice. In this context, Giddens rightly points out,

> The basic domain of the study of social sciences, according to the theory of structuration, is neither the experience of the individual actor, nor the existence of any form of societal totality, but social practices ordered across time and space (Giddens, 1984: 2).

In other words, Giddens defines social practice as the mediator between action and structure, a central concept from classical and modern sociology and philosophy, which includes agents, actions, structures, systems and power. He redefines and reformulates the ideas and concepts to become mutually dependent and combined to constitute social practices. Let us closely examine some elements combined to make up the social practice.

SOCIAL PRACTICE

Giddens claims that a society consists of social practices produced and reproduced across time and space. Consequently, Giddens finds it necessary to define social practice by using concepts that do not favour the action perspective over the structure perspective or vice versa.

Agent: Giddens starts his attempts to pin down social practice with a definition of an agent. Agents are knowledgeable about most of their connections. This wealth of knowledge is primarily expressed as *practical consciousness.* Giddens points out that we possess enough knowledge to carry out various types of action. We know the rules of conduct and the sequence of actions. These actions are routinized and take place at a practical level of consciousness.

On the other hand, he also discusses *discursive consciousness,* which differs from the practical level of consciousness. Discursive consciousness includes knowledge that we cannot immediately account for. However, for Giddens, practical knowledge seems to be the most decisive factor in understanding social life.

Agency: Unlike many classical sociologists, Giddens does not see actions as isolated phenomena. He sees action as a flow of events with a start or finish. The agency takes place with knowledge and practical consciousness. To Giddens, actions are purposive and intentional and have unintended consequences. The idea of unintended consequences plays a significant role in Gidden's theory and is especially important in getting from agency to the social system level.

STRUCTURE AND SYSTEM

In addition to 'agent' and 'action', Giddens distinguishes between *structure* and *system.* For example, every day of the year, city buses drive along the same routes; passengers get on, buy tickets, sit down and get off. These actions are constantly repeated and reproduced in a social pattern that Giddens calls a *social system.* Giddens defines a *social system* as reproduced social practices or 'reproduced relations between actors or collectivities organized as regular social practices' (Giddens, 1984: 17).

Thus, the idea of a social system is derived from Giddens's focal concern with practice. Social systems do not have structures, but they do exhibit structural properties. Social systems consist of the relation between actors or collectivities reproduced across time and space, that is, actions that are repeated and extend beyond one single action. Social systems are social practices reproduced, thus creating a pattern of social relations.

Giddens's concept of structure is mainly inspired by structuralism. He does not use the concept of structure as an external frame. According to him, the structure does not exist; it is continuously produced via agents who draw on this very structure when they act. The structure is defined as: 'the structuring properties (rules and resources) . . . the properties which make it possible for discernibly similar social practices to exist across varying periods space and which lend them systematic form' (ibid.).

The structure is made possible by the existence of rules and resources. Structures do not exist in time and space. Still, they manifest in social systems as reproduced practices. Giddens says, 'structure only exists in and through the activities of human agents'. Gidden's concept of rule refers to procedures of action. They are formulas telling us 'how to go on in social life' (ibid.: 256). The concept of resource is closely related to power as the medium through which agents can perform their 'transformative activity'.

Thus, agent, action and structure are interconnected; therefore, in Giddens's terms,

> a structure cannot be conceived as something external or 'outside of' the agent. The traditional concept of structure is dissolved and simultaneously becomes the medium for and outcome of the social practice of the agent (*Structuration Theory: Meaning and Major Features*, retrieved on 25 January 2023).

THE DUALITY OF STRUCTURE

The *duality of structure* is the very core of structuration theory. The concept of *practice* plays a key role. 'Structure is both the medium and outcome of the practices constituting social systems' (Giddens, 1981: 27).

In other words, the structure-actor relation is no longer conceived as a dualism but a duality. The concept of duality of structure connects the production of social interaction, performed by knowledgeable agents, with the reproduction of social systems across time and space (*Structuration Theory: Meaning and Major Features*, retrieved on 25 January 2023). The fact that a connection of structure has replaced the traditional concept of structure as structural properties consisting of rules and resources means that, to Giddens, the structure is no longer deterministic but both enabling and constraining. The duality of structure is the core of Giddens's conception of social practice and, thus, of his social ontology, that is, his conception of the nature of society. In this sense, society is seen as a social practice, constantly creating and recreating society in a structuration process. The duality of structure is Giddens's solution to actor-structure dualism and, thus, the basis of an adequate analysis of modern society. The entire process of the duality of structure can be represented as shown in Figure 7.1.

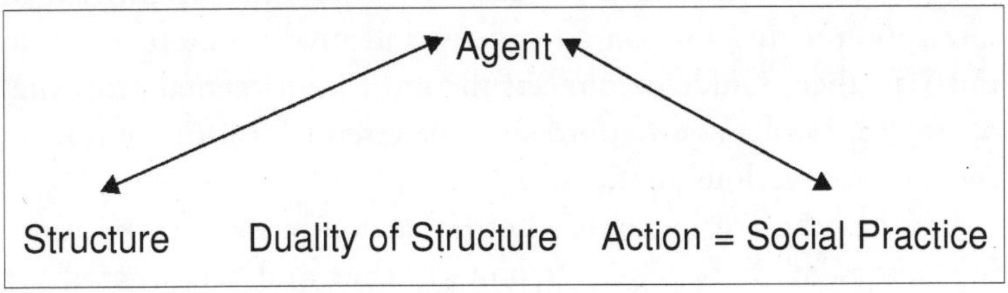

Figure 7.1: Duality of Structure

THE CONCEPT OF STRUCTURATION

The concept of structuration is based on the idea that '(t)he constitution of agents and structures are not two independently given sets of phenomena, a dualism, but represent a duality . . .

the structural properties of social systems are both medium and outcome of the practices they recursively organize' (Giddens, 1984: 25) or: 'The moment of the production of action is also one of reproduction in the contexts of the day-to-day enactment of social life' (ibid.: 26).

Structure and agency are involved in a duality rather than dualism. Hence, one cannot exist without the other. Structuration is based on the dialectical relationship between structure and agency.

In addition, Giddens also discussed the importance of time and space in structuration theory. Both depend on whether other people are present temporally or spatially. He rightly emphasized that time and space depend upon routinized and regionalized interaction, among others.

> Routinization of interaction pattern is what gives them continuity across time, thereby reproducing structure (rules and resources) and structures (institutions). At the same time, routinization gives predictability to action and, in doing so, provides for a sense of ontological security (Turner, 2002: 471).

The *ontological security system* of an agent refers to the fundamental 'force' behind much action as an unconscious set of processes to gain a 'sense of trust' in interaction with others. In other words, people realize their need for trust in others in the process of interaction across time in an orderly and predictable manner. In this way, then, Giddens connects the most fundamental properties of structure (rules and resources) to the essential features of human agents (unconscious motives).

On the other, regionalization orders action in space by positioning actors in place vis-à-vis one another and circumscribing how they present themselves and act (ibid.: 471). Therefore, the regionalization of interaction is essential to sustain broader structural patterns and ontological security of actors. With the concept of regionalization of interaction, Giddens addresses the intersection of space and time (Giddens, 1984: 110-44). Giddens introduces the idea of 'locale' to account for the physical space in which interaction occurs and the contextual knowledge about what is to happen in this space (Turner, 2002: 473). In a locale, actors not only establish their presence concerning each other but also use their stock of knowledge to interpret the context of the locale. Here, Turner summarizes:

> Regionalization of interaction through the creation of locales facilitates the maintenance of routines. In turn, maintaining routines across time and space sustains institutional structures. Thus, through routinized and regionalized interaction systems, agents' reflexive capacities operate to reproduce institutional patterns (ibid.: 474).

Giddens's theory of structuration is the synthesis of diverse theoretical traditions. His theoretical analysis involves several elements taken from different existing theoretical approaches.

The theory of structuration can be briefly outlined in the following points:

(*i*) Structuration theory is an effort to synthesize diverse theoretical traditions. Therefore, it is a more eclectic theoretical approach than any discovery.

(*ii*) Giddens's conceptualization of structure as rules and resources borrow from French structuralism. Structural analysis is thus reattached to the ongoing process of interaction.

(*iii*) The discussion of regionalization and routinization comes from Goffman's dramaturgical concepts and time-space geography. In this sense, one of Giddens's most widely recognized achievements in social theory is his effort to bring the issues of time and space to the fore. Here, the limitations of most interactionist theories are overcome.

(*iv*) The analysis of discursive and practical consciousness draws from both phenomenology and ethnomethodology, but it also connects them to interactionism and psychoanalytic theory. Giddens corrects the extremes of ethnomethodology and phenomenology and emphasizes the reflexive monitoring of actions in situations.

Unlike many others, Giddens has gone beyond a programme statement for agency-structure integration analysed, its various elements and focused on the nature of the interrelationship.

Giddens's approach to structuration is most important here, defined in inherently integrative terms.

GIDDENS'S ANALYSIS OF MODERNITY

Giddens analysed modernity in his book *The Nation-State and Violence* (1986). However, a more coherent analysis of contemporary society (*Zeitdiagnose)* was presented by him only in the 1990s. It includes an analysis of the characteristics of institutions in modern society and the specific characteristics of modern people, their self-identity and mutual relations. This analysis of contemporary culture is found in the books *The Consequences of Modernity* (1990), *Modernity and Self-Identity* (1991) and *The Transformation of Intimacy* (1992).

Giddens's analysis of modernity extends from a general discussion of social institutions and their rapid transformation to the implications for the individual and mutual interaction between institutional and personal relations. Giddens claims that the social forms of organization that developed in Europe from the start of the 1600s and onwards have become global. These forms of organization and thus 'modernity' are set in the interplay of several institutional dimensions, namely capitalism, industrialism, the surveillance and information control of the nation-state and the development of military power. However, Giddens makes a distinction between premodern and modern society. Giddens emphasizes primarily modern society's dynamic character. Modern society changes with a unique pace, scope and intensity. Premodern civilizations have also experienced change, but these are incomparable with the strength and scope of the world's changes in the past two hundred years.

The most dynamic aspects of modernity can be summarized in three points, which are pervasive themes in Giddens's analysis of modernity. These are:

1. separation of time and space;
2. the 'disembodying' mechanisms; and
3. the reflexive character of modernity.

1. *Separation of Time and Space:* The more significant part of our everyday social interaction no longer takes place simultaneously or in the same space. Unlike earlier times, when the home and village were the central places (locale), families are now scattered in time and space. For example, the father works in a neighbouring town, selling furniture for export to France through telephone, telefax and e-mail. Mother, who works as a health visitor, drives around visiting patients, but she is, via her mobile phone, in continual contact with the leader of the 24-hour care service. Their son is in the tenth class and gathers information on Ghana's infrastructure from a database for their class requirements. His older sister stays in Canada but communicates with her family via phone, airmail or e-mail. Since time has become standardized and globalized, family members can interact with each other and the surrounding world without difficulty. Not only the concept of time but also the concept of space is changing and undergoing a process of 'emptying'. Each new technological development expands our space significantly. The fact that we can be in the same space but not necessarily the same locale is one of the driving forces behind modern rational organization (Giddens, 1990: 18-19). In other words, if a modern corporation wants to function optimally, it must be able to coordinate the actions of large numbers of persons who may be separated in time and space. Giddens rightly points out, 'Living in a more globalized society. However, our lives are influenced by people who never see or meet, who may be living on the far side of the world from us' (ibid., 2004: 680).
2. *The 'Disembodying' Mechanism:* In early societies, institutions and actions were embedded in local communities before time-space separation. The condition has changed because social relations are no longer limited to the local communities but have been 'lifted out' from a regional context of interaction by disembedding mechanisms (ibid., 1990: 21). Giddens distinguishes between two types of disembedding mechanisms, *symbolic tokens* and *expert systems.* Symbolic tokens are exchange media that 'can be passed around' among individuals and institutions. Money can be considered an example of a symbolic

token. Expert systems refer to the movement of social relations from one context to another. For example, when I take the bus, I enter a vast network of expert systems enabling the construction of buses and roads and developing traffic systems. Time-space separation and disembedding mechanisms are mutually dependent.

3. *The Reflexivity of Modern Society:* Reflexivity is the third aspect of modern society, as discussed by Giddens. Reflexivity is a general feature of all human activities. As Giddens puts it, 'the reflexivity of modern social life consists in the fact that social practices are constantly examined and reformed in the light of incoming information about those very practices, thus constitutively altering their character' (Giddens, 1990: 38).

He thinks 'reflexivity' is of immense significance in grasping the production of personal and social life. 'Social reflexivity refers to thinking about or reflecting upon the circumstances in which we live our lives' (ibid., 2004: 680).

Modern society is experiencing a reflexivity process at both the institutional and personal level for creating and changing modern systems and forms of social organization reflexivity is made possible, especially by the development of mass communications. Writing started the process, but the development of other means of communication enabled societies to collect and store large amounts of information and thus raised the level of reflexivity compared to earlier times. In modernity, our actions are rarely guided by tradition and we act according to tradition only if it seems justified and rational. Marriage is a good example of reflexive orientation towards tradition and modernity. Earlier, people got married because it was a natural part of the tradition, but today, people still get married, not because of tradition, but more as part of a reflexive process. In other words, we have become able to reflect on ourselves by expanding the level of time-space distanciation. Our past, present and future become visible and are held in front of us like a mirror. This brings about a situation in which social practices are constantly investigated and changed based on newly acquired information.

These changes, like reflexivity and the role of tradition, have moved society towards what Giddens calls a post-traditional order. Tradition has become evacuated and problematized. This has implications for our ontological security.

THE CONSEQUENCES OF MODERNITY FOR ONTOLOGICAL SECURITY

The increased reflexivity of modernity creates radical doubt at both institutional and personal levels. This doubt influences our perception of trust and risk. Trust refers to the confidence we have either in individuals or in institutions. In a world of rapid transformation, traditional forms tend to dissolve. Relations of trust can be crucial to a person's development and possibilities of action and consequently, the concept of trust is vital to Giddens (Giddens, 1990: 79).

Giddens sees trust as being closely related to ontological security. For example, an infant develops the basis for ontological security about their mother and father. If an infant experiences strong, positive and primarily predictable routines with his mother, it develops a strong ontological security that protects the child against unnecessary dangers and threats. It can be said that the truest between mother and child is a kind of vaccine. Trust in systems and the risks connected with this trust are crucial for the ontological security that constitutes the basis of our identity and confidence in our social and material world.

Based on the above discussion, we have reached the point where time and space are stretched out in modernity. Social relations that previously took place in a local context are dissolved and reorganized across time and space. This distinction process globalization, which Giddens defines as an intensification of worldwide social relations that connect distant localities so that local relations and occurrences are shaped by events thousands of miles away (ibid.: 64).

In addition, Giddens subsequently developed his analysis by examining the consequences of modernity on the individual, identity, sexuality, and institutions. The central theme of his work is an analysis of the changes that endue in the interaction between the expensive social institutions and individuals in their day-to-day lives.

In short, Giddens presented a very innovative work of structuration theory and an analysis of modern society. The structure-agency 'duality' which stands at the conceptual core of Giddens's formulation of 'structuration theory', is interpreted by him as underwriting such a conclusion. Nothing is the dialect of powerlessness and empowerment in modern societies; all that can be done is identify possible 'transformation moving beyond modernity'.

KEY TERMS

Archaeology: A method of historical research aimed at the statements of discourses and statement processes (practices) whose primary purpose is to reveal the discursive rules that constitute various fields of knowledge (*The Archaeology of Knowledge*, retrieved on 25 January 2023).

Biopower: A power that has developed since the seventeenth century, which operates by disciplining individuals and regulating the population.

Deconstruction: A critical technique, especially in literary criticism, claims that there is no single innate meaning and thus no correct interpretation of a text. It involves finding out the meaning of meaning.

Discourse: Usually explained as a 'regulated order of talk', but here, it includes the concept of chains of statements, institutionalized statement processes (practices) and the historically and culturally determined rules that regulate the form and content of the order of talk.

Discursive Practice: Discursive practice can be a specific procedure of social science for developing and reproducing knowledge about an object of knowledge.

Duality of Structures: The mediating concepts that transcend the actor-structure dualism. The structure is the medium for and outcome of an actor's actions.

Episteme: A structured field of knowledge or the unreflected conditions, the historical and cultural patterns, that determines what is thought and what is conceivable during various periods.

Genealogy: A method of historical research aimed at discovering and deriving power relationships to create a foundation for criticizing contemporary phenomena.

Grammatology: A science of writing that Derrida calls 'grammatology'.

Logocentrism: Logocentrism is the search for a universal system of thought that reveals what is true, correct, beautiful and so on.

Panoptic: An all-seeing form of surveillance that can be traced back to Jeremy Bentham's idea of an 'inspection house', where from a central point, it is possible to see and monitor what is going on all around.

Plastic Sexuality: When sexuality is no longer synonymous with reproduction, it can be shaped and used to further our process of self-identity.

Power Analytics: The inductive approach to a more complex power analysis used to study biopower.

Practices: Rule-controlled actions, conduct, procedures, methods, etc., that have to do with discourses, as well as institutions and systems.

Pure Relation: A relation between two persons who enter a relationship for their own sake and stay together only as long as it is satisfactory for them to do so.

Self-identity: Not a given entity but a process. It is constantly produced and reproduced via the actor's actions.

Social Ontology: Structuration theory attempts to describe social reality and is called social ontology.

Social Practice: Society does not consist of a predetermined universe of objects. Society is constantly produced and reproduced by actively acting agents in their social practice. Social practice constitutes us as actors and simultaneously realizes and embodies structure.

REFERENCES

Cuff, E.C., W.W. Sharrock and D.W., Francis, *Perspectives in Sociology*, London: Unwin Hyman, 1990.

Derrida, Jacques, *Writing and Difference*, London: Routledge, 1978.

Foucault, Michel, *Discipline and Punish*, New York: Vintage, 1979.

——, *The History of Sexuality*, vol.1: *An Introduction*, New York: Vintage, 1980.

Giddens, Anthony, *A Contemporary Critique of Historical Materialism*, London: MacMillan, 1981.

——, *Capitalism and Modern Social Theory*, Cambridge: Cambridge University Press, 1971.

——, *New Rules of Sociological Method: A Positive Critique of Interpretative Sociologies*, New York: Basic Books, 1976.

——, *Sociology*, 4th edn., Cambridge: Polity Press, 2004.

——, *The Consequences of Modernity*, Cambridge: Polity Press, 1990.

——, *The Constitution of Society: Outline of the Theory of Structuration*, Berkeley: University of California Press, 1984.

Ritzer, George, *Post-modern Social Theory*, New York: McGraw-Hill, 1997.

——, *Sociological Theory*, Singapore: McGraw Hill Publishing Company, 1988.

Turner, Jonathan H., *The Structure of Sociological Theory*, Jaipur: Rawat Publications, 2002.

The Archaeology of Knowledge. https://kw.ukessays.com/essays/sociology/the-archeology-of-knowledge.php retrieved on 25 January 2023.

Structuration Theory: Meaning and Major Features — Your Article Library. https://www.yourarticlelibrary.com/essay/sociology-essay/structuration-theory-meaning-and-major-features/39914 retrieved on 25 January 2023.

Bibliography

Abraham, Francis and J.H. Morgan, *Sociological Thought From Comte to Sorokin,* Chennai: Macmillan, 1985.

Abraham, Francis M., *Modern Sociological Theory: An Introduction,* Kolkata: Oxford University Press, 2000.

Abraham, J.H., *Origins and Growth of Sociology,* New York: Penguin Books, 1977.

Alexander, Jeffrey, 'The 'Individualist Dilemma', in Phenomenology and Interactionism' in S.N. Eisenstadt and H.J. Helle (eds.), *Macro-Sociological Theory,* vol. 1, London: Sage, 1985.

——, *Theoretical Logic in Sociology,* vol. 1, *Positivism, Presuppositions and Current Controversies,* Berkeley: University of California Press, 1982.

Alexander, Jeffrey and Paul Colomy, 'Toward Neofunctionalism', *Sociological Theory,* 3, 1985.

Althusser, Louis, *For Marx,* Harmondsworth: Penguin, 1969.

——, *Politics and History,* London: NLB, 1977.

Althusser, Louis and Etienne Balibar, *Reading Capital,* London: New Left Books, 1970.

Aron, Raymond, *German Sociology* (trans. Mary and Thomas Bottormore), New York: Free Press, 1967.

——, *Main Currents in Sociological Thought,* vol. 1, New York: Penguin Books, 1965.

——, *Main Currents in Sociological Thought,* vol. 2, Garden City: Doubleday, 1970.

Bales, Robert Freed, *Interaction Process Analysis,* Cambridge, Massachusetts: Addison-Wesley, 1950.

Beck, Lewis White, 'Neo-Kantianism', *The Encyclopedia of Philosophy,* vol. 5, New York: Macmillan, 1967.

Benedix, Reinhard and Seymour Martin Lipset, *Class, Status and Power,* New York: Free Press, 1966.

Benton, Ted, *The Rise and Fall of Structural Marxism: Althusser and his Influence,* New York: St. Martin's, 1984.

Berger, Peter L., *The Sacred Canopy,* New York: Doubleday, 1969.

Berger, Peter L. and Thomas Luckmann, *The Social Construction of Reality,* New York: Doubleday and Co, Inc., 1967.

Bierstedt, Robert, *American Sociological Theory: A Critical History*, London: Academic Press, 1981.

——, *The Social Order*, New York: McGraw-Hill, Inc., 1974.

Black, 'Review of Social Theories of Talcott Parsons', *Journal of Philosophy*, 59, 29 March 1962.

Bleicher, Josef (ed.), *Contemporary Hermeneutics: Hermeneutics as Method, Philosophy and Critique*, London: Routledge and Kegan Paul, 1980.

Blumer, Herbert, 'Society as Symbolic Interaction', in A. Ross (ed.), *Human Behaviour and Social Processes*, Boston: Houghton Mifflin, 1962.

Bottomore, T.B., 'Karl Mark: Sociologist or Marxist?' in *Theories and Paradigms in Contemporary Sociology*, Serge Denisoff et al., Itasca: F.E. Peacock Publishers, Inc., 1974.

——, *Sociology: A Guide to Problems and Literature*, Bombay: Blackie and Son Ltd., 1975.

Bottomore, Thomas B., *Marxist Sociology*, London: Macmillan, 1975.

Bottomore, T., 'Out of this World', *New York Review of Books*, 6 November 1969.

Bruun, H.H., *Science, Values and Politics in Max Weber's Methodology*, Copenhagen: Munksgaard, 1972.

Burger, Thomas, *Max Weber's Theory of Concept Formation: History, Laws and Ideal Types*, Durham: Duke University Press, 1976.

Cicourel, Aron V., *Cognitive Sociology*, London: Macmillan, 1973.

Cohen, G.A., *Karl Marx's Theory of History*, Princeton: Princeton University Press, 1978.

Colletti, Locio, *Marxism and Hegel*, London: Verso, 1979.

Collins, Randall and Michael Makowsky, *The Discovery of Society*, New York: Random House, 1972.

Comte, Auguste, *Course de Philosophic Positive* (*The Course of Positivist Philosophy or the Positive Philosophy*), translated and condensed by Harriet Martineau, London: Trübner, 1853.

——, *System de Politique Positive* (*System of Positive Polity* or *Positive Polity*), Four Volumes, Paris: Cress, 1912.

Coser, Lewis A., *Masters of Sociological Thought*, Jaipur: Rawat Publications, 1997.

——, (ed.), *The Idea of Social Structure: Papers in Honour of Robert K. Merton*, New York: Harcourt Brace Jovanovich, 1975.

Craib, Ian, *Classical Social Theory: An Introduction to the Thought of Marx, Weber, Durkheim and Simmel*, New York: Oxford University Press, 1997.

Cuff, E.C., W.W. Sharrock and D.W. Francis, *Perspectives in Sociology*, London: Unwin Hyman, 1990.

Derrida, Jacques, *Writing and Difference,* London: Routledge, 1978.

Dickens, David, 'Phenomenology', in *Theoretical Perspectives in Sociology*, Scott McNall (ed.), New York: St. Martin's Press, 1979.

Durkheim, E., *The Rules of Sociological Method,* New York: Free Press, [1895] 1938.

——, *Suicide,* New York: Free Press, [1897] 1951.

——, *The Elementary Forms of Religious Life,* New York: Free Press, [1912] 1965.

——, *The Division of Labour in Society*, New York: Free Press, 1964.

Ellwood, C.A., *A History of Social Philosophy*, 1955.

Engels, Friedrich, *Anti Duhring*, Peking: Foreign Language Press, [1878] 1976.

Foucault, Michel, *Discipline and Punish,* New York: Vintage, 1979.

——, *The History of Sexuality*, vol. 1: *An Introduction,* New York: Vintage, 1980.

Frank, R.I., Translator's introduction to Max Weber, *The Agrarian Sociology of Ancient Civilisations,* London: NLB, 1976.

Garfinkel, Harold, *Studies in Ethnomethodology*, Englewood Cliffs: Prentice-Hall, Inc., 1967.

Giddens, Anthony, *A Contemporary Critique of Historical Materialism,* London: Macmillan, 1981.

——, *Capitalism and Modern Social Theory*, Cambridge: Cambridge University Press, 1971.

——, *New Rules of Sociological Method: A Positive Critique of Interpretive Sociologies,* New York: Basic Books, 1976.

——, *Sociology*, 4th edn., Oxford: Polity Press, 2004.

——, *The Consequences of Modernity*, Cambridge: Polity Press, 1990.

——, *The Constitution of Society: Outline of the Theory of Structuration,* Berkeley: University of California Press, 1984.

Goffman, Erving, 'The Interaction Order', *American Sociological Review*, 48, February 1983.

——, *The Presentation of Self in Everyday Life,* 2nd edn., Harmondsworth: Penguin, 1959.

Gorman, Robert A., 'Phenomenology and Methodology of Social Science: The Origins' in *The Classical Tradition in Sociology: The European Tradition,* Raymond Boudon, Mohamed Cherkaoui and Jeffrey Alexander (eds.), vol. III, London: Sage Publications, 1997.

Habermas, Jürgen, *Legitimation Crisis,* Boston: Beacon Press, 1975.

——, *The Theory of Communicative Action,* two vols., Boston: Beacon Press, 1984.

——, *Toward a Rational Society,* Boston: Beacon Press, 1970.

Handel, Warren H., *Contemporary Sociological Theory,* Englewood Cliffs: Prentice-Hall, Inc., 1993.

Haralambos, M., *Sociology: Themes and Perspectives,* New Delhi: Oxford University Press, New Delhi, 1999.

Hearn, F., *Reason and Freedom in Sociological Thought,* Boston: Allen and Unwin, 1985.

Hegel, G.W.F., *Philosophy of Right,* Oxford: Clarendon Press, 1958.

Heritage, John, *Garfinkel and Ethnomethodology,* Cambridge: Polity Press, 1984.

Howe, Irving (ed.), *Essential Works of Socialism,* New York: Rinehart and Winston, 1971.

Husserl, Edmund, *Ideas: General Introduction to Pure Phenomenology* (trans. W.R. Boyce Gibson), New York: Humanities Press, 1931.

Johnson, Benton, *Functionalism in Modern Sociology: Understanding Talcott Parsons,* Morristown: General Learning Press, 1975.

Jordan, Z.A., *The Evolution of Dialectical Materialism,* New York: St. Martin's Press, 1967.

Kalberg, Stephen, 'Max Weber's Types of Rationality: Cornerstones for the Analysis of Rationalisation Process in History', *American Journal of Sociology,* 85, 1980.

Larson, Calvin J., *Major Themes in Sociological Theory,* New York: David Mckay, 1973.

Lefebvre, Henri, *The Sociology of Marx,* New York: Vintage, 1981.

Loomis, Charles and Zona K. Loomis, *Modern Social Theories,* Princeton: D. Van Nostrand Company, 1965.

Lukacs, George, *History and Class Consciousness,* New York: MIT Press, [1922] 1968.

Lukes, S., *Emile Durkheim: His Life and Work,* Standard: Stanford University Press, 1973.

Manning Phil, 'Drama as Life: The Significance of Goffman's Changing Use of the Theatrical Metaphor. In *The Classical Tradition in Sociology: The American Tradition,* Jeffrey Alexander, Raymond Boudon and Mohamed Cherkaoui (eds.), vol. IV, London: Sage Publications, 1997.

Marx, Karl and F. Engels, *Collected Works,* New York: International Publishers, 1975.

——, *The German Ideology,* New York: International Publishers, [1846] 1947.

——, *The Holy Family, or Critique of Critical Criticism,* Moscow: Progress Publishers, [1845] 1956.

——, 'The Class Struggle', in *Social Change,* Amitai Etzioni and Eva Etzioni-Halevy (eds.), New York: Basic Books, 1973.

Marx, Karl, *A Contribution to the Critique of Political Economy,* Moscow: Progress Publishers, [1859] 1977.

——, *A Critique of Hegel's Philosophy of Right,* J O'Malley (ed.), Cambridge: Cambridge University Press, [1843] 1970.

——, *Capital,* London: Lawrence and Wishart, 1970.

——, *Early Writings,* translated and edited by T.B. Bottomore, New York: McGraw-Hill, 1964.

——, *Grundrisse: Foundations of the Critique of Political Economy,* Middlesex: Penguin, [1953] 1973.

——, *Selected Writings in Sociology and Social Philosophy,* translated by T.B. Bottomore, London: McGraw-Hill, 1964.

——, *The Economic and Philosophic Manuscripts of 1844,* New York: International Publishers, [1932] 1964.

Meek, R., *Studies in the Labour Theory of Value,* Lawrence & Wishart, London, 1973.

Mehan, Hugh and Houston Wood, *The Reality of Ethnomethodology,* New York: Wiley, 1975.

Merton, Robert K. and Alice S. Kitt, 'Contribution to the Theory of Reference Group Behaviour', in *The Classical Tradition in Sociology: The American Tradition,* Jeffrey et al. (eds.), vol. II, London: Sage Publications, 1997.

Merton, Robert K., 'Introduction to Social Theory and Social Structure', in *The Classical Tradition in Sociology: The American Tradition,* Jeffrey Alexander, Raymond Boudon and Mohamed Cherkaoui (eds.), volume II, London: Sage Publications, 1997.

——, *Social Theory and Social Structure,* New York: Free Press, 1957.

Mitchel, G. Duncan (ed.), *A New Dictionary of Sociology,* London: Routledge, 1999.

Morrison, Ken, *Marx, Durkheim, Weber: Formation of Modern Social Thought,* London: Sage Publication, 1995.

Mueller-Vollmer, Kurt, 'Language, Mind and Artifact: An Outline of Hermeneutic Theory Since the Enlightenment', in *The Hermeneutics Reader, K. Muller-Vollmer* (ed.), New York: Continuum.

Orru, Marco, *Review of Talcott Parsons: On Economy and Society* (by Robert J. Holton and Bryan S. Turner) and *The Integration of Economic and Sociological Theory,* The Marshall Lectures, Cambridge: University of Cambridge, 1953.

Parsons, Talcott and Edward A. Shills, *Toward a General Theory of Action,* Cambridge: Harvard University Press, 1951.

Parsons, Talcott, 'An Outline of the Social System', in *Theories of Society,* Talcott Parsons, Edward Shils, Kaspar Naegele and Jesse Pitts (eds), vol. I, New York: Free Press, 1965.

——, 'Evolutionary Universals in Society', *American Social Review,* 29 (1964), pp. 339-57.

——, 'On Building Social System Theory: A Personal History', in *Social Systems and the Evolution of Action Theory,* New York: Free Press, 1977.

——, 'Social Interaction', in *International Encyclopedia of the Social Science,* David Sills (ed.), vol. 7, New York: Macmillan, 1968.

——, 'Some Comments on the State of the General Theory of Action', *American Sociological Review,* 18 December 1953: 618-31.

——, 'The Structure of Social Action', in *The Classical Tradition in Sociology: The American Tradition,* Jeffrey Alexander, Raymond Boudon and Mohamed Cherkaoui (eds.), volume II, London: Sage Publications, 1997.

——, *Social System and the Evolution of Action Theory,* New York: Free Press, 1977.

——, *Societies: Evolutionary and Comparative Perspectives,* Englewood Cliff: Prentice-Hall, Inc., 1966.

——, *The Social System,* New York: Free Press, 1951.

——, *The Structure of Social Action,* New York: McGraw Hill, 1937.

——, *The System of Modern Societies,* Englewood Cliffs: Prentice-Hall Inc., 1971.

Peel, J.D.Y., *Herbert Spencer: The Evolution of a Sociologist,* London: Heinemann, 1971.

Pope, Whitney, *Durkheim's Suicide: A Classic Analyzed,* Chicago: University of Chicago Press, 1976.

Rex, John, *Key Problems in Sociological Theory,* London: Routledge and Kegan Paul, 1961.

Ricardo, D., *On the Principles of Political Economy and Taxation,* Kitchener: Batoche Books, [1817] 2001.

Rickert, Heinrich, *Science and History: A Critique of Positivist Epistemology* (trans. George Reisman), D. Van Nostrand, Princeton, 1962.

Ritzer, George, *Postmodern Social Theory,* New York: McGraw-Hill, 1997.

——, *Sociological Theory,* Singapore: McGraw-Hill Company, 1988.

Robey, David (ed.), *Structuralism: An Introduction,* Oxford: Oxford University Press, 1973.

Rossides, Daniel W., *The History and Nature of Sociological Theory,* Boston: Houghton Mifflin Company, 1978.

Rotenstreich, Nathan, *Basic Problems of Marx's Philosophy,* Indianapolis: Bobb Merrill, 1965.

Rubel, M. and M. Manale, *Marx Without Myth: A Chronological Study of His Life and Work,* New York: Harper & Row, 1975.

Schutz, Alfred, *Collected Papers*, vol. I, edited by Maurice Natanson and Martinus Mijhoff, The Haque, 1962.

——, *The Phenomenology of the Social World*, Evanston: Northwestern University Press, [1932] 1967.

Scruton, R., *A Dictionary of Political Thought*, London: Pan Books, 1982.

Shills, Edward A., Robert Freed Bales and Talcott Parsons, *Working Papers in the Theory of Action*, New York: Free Press, 1953.

Smith, A., *The Wealth of Nations*. W. Strahan and T. London: Cadell, 1776.

Spencer, Herbert, 'The Development Hypothesis', in *Essays: Scientific, Political and Speculative*, vol. 1, New York: Appleton, [1852] 1915.

——, *The Principles of Ethics*, two volumes, New York: Appleton, [1892-93] 1914.

——, 'Progress: Its Law and Cause', in *Essays: Scientific, Political and Speculative*, vol. 1, New York: Appleton, [1857] 1915.

——, 'The Development Hypothesis', vol. 1 in *Essays: Scientific, Political and Speculative*, New York: Appleton, [1852] 1915.

——, 'The Social Organism', in *Essays: Scientific, Political and Speculative*, volume II, New York: Appleton, [1857] 1915.

——, *An Autobiography*, 2 vols., London: Watts, London, [1904] 1926.

——, *Education: Intellectual, Moral and Physical*, Paterson: Littlefield, N.J. [1854-9] 1963.

——, *First Principles*, New York: Dewitt Revolving Fund, [1862] 1958.

——, *Social Statics: the conditions of human happiness specified and the first of them developed*, London: Routledge, [1850] 1954.

——, *The Man Versus the State*, 2nd edn., London: Watts , [1884] 1950.

——, *The Principles of Sociology*, 3 vols., New York: Appleton, [1876-96] 1925-9.

——, *The Study of Sociology*, Ann Arbor: University of Michigan Press, [1873] 1961.

Thompson, K. and J. Junstall (eds.), *Sociological Perspectives*, Middlesex: Penguin Books.

Timasheff, Nicholas, S., *Sociological Theory: Its Nature and Growth*, Third Edition, New York: Random House, 1967.

Tribe, Keith (ed.), *Reading Weber*, London: Routledge, 1989.

Troeltch, Ernst, *The Social Teaching of the Christian Churches*, London: Allen and Unwin, 1956.

Tucker, R.C., *Marx-Engels Reader*, New York: W.W. Norton, 1978.

Turner, Jonathan H., *The Structure of Sociological Theory*, Jaipur: Rawat Publications, 2002.

——, *The Structure of Sociological Theory*, Homewood: The Dorsey Press, 1978.

Turner, Roy (ed.), *Ethnomethodology: Selected Readings,* Baltimore: Penguin Books, 1974.

Wallace, Ruth A. and Alison Wolf, *Contemporary Sociological Theory: Continuing The Classical Tradition,* Englewood Cliffs: Prentice-Hall, Inc., 1980.

Weber, Marianne, *Max Weber: A Biography,* New York: John Wiley & Sons, 1975.

Weber, Max, 'Objectivity in Social Science and Social Policy', in *Max Weber: The Methodology of the Social Sciences,* E.A. Shills and H. Finch (eds.), New York: Free Press, 1949.

——, *Economy and Society,* 3 vols., Totowa: Bedminster Press, [1921] 1968.

——, *Economy and Society,* G. Roth and C. Wittich (eds.), Berkeley: University of California Press, 1978.

——, *General Economic History,* New York: Collier Books, [1922] 1961.

——, *Roscher and Knies: The Logical Problems of Historical Economics* (trans. Guy Oakes), New York: The Free Press, 1975.

——, *The Methodology of the Social Sciences* (trans. and ed. Edward A. Shills and Henry A. Finch), Chicago: Free Press, 1949.

——, *The Protestant Ethic and the Spirit of Capitalism,* New York: Scribner's, [1904-5] 1958.

——, *The Theory of Social and Economic Organization* (trans. and edited by A.M. Henderson and Talcott Parsons), New York: Free Press, 1964.

——, *The Theory of Social and Economic Organization,* London & New York: Oxford University Press, 1947.

Weigert Andrew, *Sociology of Everyday Life,* New York: Longman, 1981.

Wiley, Thomas E., *Back to Kant: The Revival of Kantianism in German Social and Historical Thought, 1860-1914,* Detroit: Wayne State University Press, 1978.

Wilson, Thomas P., 'Normative and Interpretive Paradigms in Sociology', in Jack Douglas (ed.), *Understanding Everyday Life,* Chicago: Aldine, 1970.

Wiltshire, David, *The Social and Political Thought of Herbert Spencer,* Oxford Historical Monograph, Oxford: Oxford University Press, 1978.

Index